THE
BUSINESS
SIDE
OF WRITING

Russell A. Stultz

PRENTICE-HALL, INC., Englewood Cliffs, New Jersey 07632

Library of Congress Cataloging in Publication Data

Stultz, Russell Allen.
  The business side of writing.

  Includes index.
  1. Technical writing.   I. Title.
T11.S725   1984   808'0666'0068   84-6825
ISBN   0-13-107822-4
ISBN   0-13-107814-3 (pbk.)

Cover design: Ben Santora
Manufacturing buyer: Ed O'Dougherty

Printed in the United States of America

10 9 8 7 6 5 4 3 2 1

ISBN 0-13-107822-4   01

ISBN 0-13-107814-3 {PBK}

Prentice-Hall International, Inc., *London*
Prentice-Hall of Australia Pty. Limited, *Sydney*
Editora Prentice-Hall do Brasil, Ltda., *Rio de Janeiro*
Prentice-Hall Canada Inc., *Toronto*
Prentice-Hall of India Private Limited, *New Delhi*
Prentice-Hall of Japan, Inc., *Tokyo*
Prentice-Hall of Southeast Asia Pte. Ltd., *Singapore*
Whitehall Books Limited, *Wellington, New Zealand*

Contents

Preface

1
About this Book

2

Tools of the Trade   15

3

Organizing Your Work   31

4

Project Research   41

5

Cost Estimating   55

6

Publications Contract Negotiations   83

7

Cost Control and Reporting   97

Publications Quality
Control Provisions   111

Publications Production   125

10

Publications Configuration and Change Control   151

11

Writing, Publications Management, and Publications Production Automation 161

Index 187

Preface

This book is a combination of several personal interests. A background in professional writing, publications supervision and management, and consulting experience in office automation, word processing, and computer systems has promoted the desire to share experiences and a few of the "tricks" learned along the way.

The intent of this book is to supply some guidelines, "how to's," "when to's," and "why's" to those who are in the writing field seeking information that will serve as a basis for advancement.

If you are not presently a writer, but enjoy painting pictures with words, then this book may interest you in a lifetime of challenging, enjoyable work and financial security. However, there is more to career writing than writing itself.

Project planning, efficient information collection, accurate cost estimating, timely cost control, an understanding of publications contracts, and a knowledge of production and quality control processes involved in producing a final publications product are all important. These, coupled with the power of a modern computer system, can provide impetus for personal growth and the success of your company.

1

About this Book

INTRODUCTION

This book is for professional technical writers, technical writing supervisors, and publications department managers. If you are interested in investigating technical writing as a career field, then the book is probably right for you too.

This is not a "how to write" book. There are already plenty of these on the market. But there are not very many books about *The Business Side of Technical Writing.*

As a past technical writer, supervisor, and manager of a large publications department for Texas Instruments, and as the chief executive officer of a "high-tech" publishing company, I have always wanted to write a book about technical publications project management.

I could spend my time writing other books that have a broader market appeal. After all, the market for a technical writer's project management book is not very big. But, because I have never been able to find enough time personally to coach my staff in the why's, when's, how's, and who's of publications project planning, development, and production, I decided to write this book.

Busy managers are frustrated with not having enough hours in a day. If we are thoughtful, we put together orientation programs to help introduce our people to the methodologies involved in our business. However, information learned in a classroom fades quickly. According to instructional theorists, classroom instruction is good for about eight hours. The way to overcome this problem is to provide a *job aid* that can be used on a continuous basis—a ready reference. It is hoped that this book can help. I, for one, plan to give this book to my staff members with the expectation that it will answer many of their questions about the business. If they use it as intended, it should organize their approach to such things as project planning, cost estimating, project research, and financial control. And it will help them to understand the publications production process and the need for publications quality control. They should have a much clearer idea of how books are produced and why quality control is important.

The book also examines ways in which modern technology can be applied to make the publications planning, development, and production processes more productive. Here publication department managers can see how computers can be applied to improve productivity in many facets of their business. Word processing, financial analysis and reporting, and production control applications are described.

If you are a new technical writer or someone who aspires to enter the technical writing profession, the book will answer many questions for you, including

- What is a career like in the technical writing profession?
- What are some of the basic tools needed by a professional writer?
- How can I organize a writing project?

If you have been in technical writing for a few years and you are getting ready to assume supervisory responsibility, you will probably be interested in answers to

- What are the costs involved in preparing and producing a book?
- How should I prepare for negotiating publications contract terms and conditions with customer representatives?
- How can I monitor and report publications project costs?

Whether you are a new technical writer or even a fiction writer, you will want the answers to some of these questions:

- What are some good publications research techniques?
- How can I increase my writing productivity?
- What are the steps a publication has to go through after it leaves my desk as manuscript?

If your product publications are constantly being revised as a result of design changes to the products they describe, you will certainly want some ideas that answer the question

- How can I prevent throwing away those expensive copies in inventory? This is where information on publications configuration control techniques may come in handy.

If you are a publications department manager looking for increased productivity for you and your staff, you will want answers to these questions:

- How can I increase technical writing throughput? Is there a way I can make financial planning quicker, easier, and more accurate?
- Are there any microcomputer-based applications that can be used to manage my production control?

WHAT THE BOOK DOES NOT DO

This book deals with professional writing as a career field. It addresses tools, techniques, methodologies, and processes; it stresses writing productivity throughout. It does not instruct the reader in grammar, parallelism, procedure writing, style, or any of the other hundreds of things needed to set down coherent words on paper. The book will touch on outlining and some of the other fundamental disciplines needed in getting a writing project organized. But it does not tell you how to write; the assumption is that you know how to write. With the ability to write, you should be ready to put your talent to work. That is where this book begins.

The hope is that the information contained in this book will make you a valuable resource to your employer. If it does, it will be beneficial to you by advancing your career in technical writing.

THE WORK AND REWARDS OF A TECHNICAL WRITER

Technical writing can be one of the most fascinating jobs in existence if you are the kind of person who likes a continual challenge and the opportunity to expand your knowledge on a daily basis. Technical writers do extensive research in new product areas. In high-technology companies, writers find themselves at the leading edge of technology, learning and describing new breakthroughs as they happen. The diversity of work is often amazing. A single writer may find himself or herself researching and describing electronic circuits, electro-mechanical interlock systems, and cryogenics all between the covers of one technical manual. The work can be a constant intellectual challenge. Of course, there are those who prefer a more leisurely pace. They can write simple operating procedures, develop product support literature including parts catalogs, or perhaps work on computer applications software reference manuals. Others delight in writing product merchandising material. Whatever your taste, there is probably a job in the writing field that suits you.

The rewards in technical writing, aside from a satisfying, challenging job, include good pay and respect from others in industry for the talents that qualify you to be a writer. The pay is competitive with other professions in industry. Most companies pay their technical writers on the same scale as other professional personnel including engineers. Good writers are so hard to find and keep that some companies have established special career paths for writers, allowing them to advance in pay as individual contributors without having to go though the supervisory and management ladder to earn attractive salaries.

In summary, a career in technical writing can be challenging and satisfying work that demands excellent pay. It is up to you to join the company that offers an intellectual challenge and a pay structure that is equal to the commitment and energy you are willing to invest.

THE PROFESSIONAL WRITER'S BACKGROUND

Where do writers come from? They come from nearly everywhere. Typically, they are people who are fast learners and good written communicators. Being a fast learner is a key attribute. Good writers must become temporary experts with the subject matter being described. They certainly must know more about the subject than they write; a good solid background is vital to doing a good job of describing a complex subject to a reader. The majority of technical writers have technical backgrounds that help them to understand the subjects they describe.

Technical writers often come from the ranks of electronic technicians, computer programmers; electrical, chemical, aeronautical, and mechanical engineers; mathematicians; and physicists. Some enter the field directly from college with engineering, English, or journalism degrees. A small number have technical writing degrees.

There is a large demand for individuals who have both a technical background and academic credentials or on-the-job experience in the technical writing field. For instance, someone who has worked as an electronic technician and has obtained a degree in journalism or English would be an ideal candidate for a writing job in an electronic equipment manufacturing company.

Technical Writer Employers

Regardless of an individual's specific theoretical education, there is an excellent demand for technical writers in industry. Almost every company that manufactures a product made up of several parts requires operating instructions, maintenance procedures, parts information, and a host of other kinds of documentation to make the product usable to the customer. In addition to the literature that supports the product once it is in the hands of the end user, there are often large quantities of reports, specifications, and assembly documentation that must be written when the product is in the design stage. If the product is to be procured by a governmental agency or a large corporation with strict procurement specification requirements, the reports and design specifications may far outweigh the operation and maintenance documentation.

Automotive, aircraft, electrical, and electronic product companies, just to name a few, all employ large numbers of technical writers. Since the technology varies widely in an aircraft company, the backgrounds of the writers vary. You may find writers who specialize in electrical, electronic, mechanical hydraulic, pneumatic, or aeronautical engineering.

Computer companies look for writers who have an understanding of digital computer architecture and software principles or perhaps even a degree in computer science. Aircraft and automotive companies look for a variety of technical backgrounds because their products feature electro-mechanical, mechanical, electrical, electronic, hydraulic, and pneumatic systems that all must be designed, operated, and serviced.

Certain companies specialize in selling the services of professional writers. These companies, sometimes called "job shops," often enter into contracts with equipment manufacturers to provide turnkey product publications. They often offer the services of professional writers to work on a temporary basis at the manufacturing location. On large aircraft or military contracts where large peaks in the work force are anticipated for a relatively short duration (i.e., from one to three years), it is common to find as many as a hundred contract writers in the work force.

Differences Between Technical Writers and Editors

There is a distinct difference between writers and editors in terms of their backgrounds and the abilities they bring to the job. The distinction is fundamentally that a technical writer has sufficient theoretical background to enable the writing of a technical manual with limited dependence on the responsible subject-matter experts for technical fundamentals, whereas an editor is basically dependent on the subject matter expert for written manuscript or extensive verbal inputs. The true writer removes the documentation burden from the company's technical staff; the editor, on the other hand, requires dedicated support from the technical staff.

Some companies use a writer-editor team, where the writer is fundamentally a technical researcher who develops a rough manuscript. The editor converts the rough manuscript into a product suitable for publication. Of course, this takes two people and is not nearly as efficient as a technical writer who has the ability to research, write the material, and edit "on the fly," producing text that is in a form suitable for publication.

Many companies employ what are often referred to as "production editors." Production editors basically take the writer's manuscript and see that it flows smoothly through the production process. They often start by ensuring that the book complies with prevailing format specifications. They may be involved with production scheduling and can help to specify type styles to be used, illustration and table locations, and other production considerations that are certainly necessary to the delivery of a quality publication.

Both the editor and production editor are important to every publications effort. Editors are often those people who are best qualified to handle a company's internal communications and newsletters. They are not, however, the best choice for writing technical manuals that contain theory, maintenance procedures, or detailed operating instructions. This is especially true when the material must describe the operation of sophisticated, high-technology equipment.

WRITING PRODUCTIVITY

Experienced writers are normally more productive than are inexperienced ones simply because the former learned many tricks of the trade. It is common for experienced writers to turn out two or three times more material than one who is new to the profession.

Measuring writer productivity is relatively easy. The index is most often usable text pages. Note the word "usable." It is possible for a writer to churn out piles of useless paper. If the material requires extensive rework and editing time, overall writer output is low. This is a case where using pages produced as an indicator of productivity is misleading. All input time must be considered to compute a writer's actual productivity. The writer who generates a modest quantity of "golden text" that flows right into the production shop with virtually no editing is worth several of those who produce stacks of poorly written text.

Writer productivity is an issue about which good professional writers are sensitive. They know that it is a measure of personal value and professional worth. For this reason, productivity is included in several different contexts throughout this book. Chapters 4, 7, and 8 address writer productivity in different ways. Chapter 5 discusses the establishment of standard costs, which embraces the concept of work unit output including writer-produced page units.

Chapter 7 deals with cost measurement, which quantifies overall productivity of a group including the writer's contribution. Chapter 10 highlights some writing automation tools, including word processing systems and dictation equipment, that can be used to make a writer more productive. The last section of Chapter 9 describes productivity measurement from a manager's point of view and makes some suggestions on improvement through both automation and motivation.

THE IMPORTANCE OF HUMAN RELATIONS IN WRITING

Writers depend on others as sources of information. They must obtain documentation and technical descriptions from those who design new products or produce and maintain engineering documentation. Without the help of these people, writers cannot function. This means that one of the personal traits of writers must be diplomacy. If a writer handles personal relations poorly, people will avoid him. If he is friendly, cooperative, and considerate, it will make his job significantly easier. Chapter 2 describes this trait in more detail.

PRIDE OF AUTHORSHIP

Professional writers know that they are subject to criticism from almost anyone who has ever read a book, much less written one. Books are almost always reviewed by at least one person, the editor, if not by a whole team of reviewers. This is where professionalism is important. The inexperienced writer has a tendency to take criticism personally. Many long, unproductive hours are spent bickering over simple changes. The professional writer takes the inputs as suggestions for improvement, moderates them in a diplomatic way, and gets the job done with a minimum amount of haggling.

The writer whose feelings are hurt by reviewers' comments is in the wrong business. Criticism "comes with the territory." If you are to finish a job on schedule and within budget, accept the criticism positively, evaluate it objectively, and get on with it. You will not only do a better job, but you will also gain the admiration of those with whom you work.

DOCUMENTATION INTEGRITY

It is imperative that a writer's work is accurate. Writers are easily measured in terms of credibility. Practically everything done is in black and white. Mistakes have a way of "coming back to roost." Any writer who has regard for a professional reputation conscientiously checks his or her work to be sure that it is right. Errors not only show a lack of thoroughness, they can be costly to the company. A product can be rendered virtually useless when the installation or operating instructions are wrong. In the case of some products, bad information can pose a threat to life. A poorly written aircraft flight manual, for example, could result in a tragic aviation accident.

A writer's words are his or her report card. If the words are accurate and easy to understand, the writer gets a good grade. If they are wrong, ambiguous, or vague to the point of confusion, the writer fails the course.

THE PUBLICATIONS ENVIRONMENT

All writers should know in the beginning that they are working in a deadline business. It can be an environment of severe pressure, particularly when the equipment or software being described is changing by the minute. Describing a "moving target" is commonplace in an era of new, untested technologies and governmental regulations that often force manufacturers to go through complete redesigns.

In addition to redesign problems, timing is often a major contributor to frustration. Starting too soon on a writing project is probably one of the most common mistakes made. The story usually goes something like this.

A book is needed for a product that is scheduled for completion in six months. The writing project estimate says the book should take four months to write and two months to typeset and print. This implies that a writer should be assigned to the project and the work started right away. However, the engineering people have staffing problems and the product design is still not firm.

The writer begins by finding the project in a state of disarray. He "spins his wheels" for a few months while the design people get their act together. To pacify him, he is given preliminary engineering drawings and product specifications that turn out to be fiction. Everything he does is scrapped. Two to three person-months of effort go down the drain, the writer is frustrated, and the entire program suffers a financial setback.

The moral of this story is to wait for the design to settle down before making a long-term writing commitment. A few checks with the right questions will tell you to hold off until the writer's time can be spent productively.

SUMMARY

Nobody has all the answers, including a technical writer, who, as mentioned early in this chapter, is a person who must become a temporary expert on the subject matter he or she is describing. If you do not have all the answers, the next best thing is having the right questions. Here is where good technical writers shine. They know the right questions and get the information required in an efficient, diplomatic way.

The few tips contained in this chapter are based on two decades of experience in the writing business. Similar tips are provided in the following chapters in addition to suggestions on tools and methodologies that can help anyone in the writing business get the job done more efficiently.

REVIEW QUESTIONS

1. What are some of the rewards associated with the writing profession?

2. What important attributes should a technical writer possess?

3. Where are technical writers typically employed?

4. What is a major difference between technical writers and editors?

5. How can a writer and editor work as a team?

6. What is a *production editor*?

7. How can a writer's productivity be measured?

8. Why is diplomacy an important trait of a writer?

9. What is *pride of authorship* and how can it be counterproductive?

10. Describe a potential problem that stems from starting a writing project too early in the development of a new product.

2

Tools of the Trade

INTRODUCTION

This chapter describes some of the basic tools that professional writers should have to help them make the most of their time. The tools include a variety of equipment and reference materials that can be used to produce both words and graphics with relative ease.

KNOWING YOUR WAY AROUND

Before beginning a writing project, you should know what has been done in the past on the same or similar efforts. You should know where the equipment is being built or where system prototypes are installed and operating; know the responsible engineering, drafting, and manufacturing people; obtain all available system documentation; and just as important, get on the drawing and specification distribution list so that you will automatically receive information on design changes. Without this information, you may wind up wasting your time describing history.

SPECIFICATIONS, STANDARDS, STATEMENTS OF WORK, AND STYLE GUIDES

Specifications, standards, statements of work, and style guides are important tools that every writer should have readily available. This section describes the uses of these important documents.

Specifications

Every seasoned technical writer collects specifications. These are a "must" if you are to understand precisely what is required to write a book. Specifications contain the content requirements and detail of technical coverage required and provide examples of text and illustrations. If the book is not written in strict compliance with the governing specification, there is a good chance that extensive rework will be required.

When using specifications, it is necessary to understand the intent as well as the letter of the specification. More important, it is essential to understand the customer's interpretation. It is always a good practice to have an early meeting with the customer to determine just what he or she thinks the specification and statement of work mean. You may find that the customer's interpretation is more liberal than your own, which can save time and money for your company. On the other hand, if the customer is a "stickler" for strict compliance, you had better know this early enough to prevent unproductive rework.

In any case, have all governing documentation, read it, understand it, and know what the customer wants before you make a large investment of time and effort.

Many writing departments, company libraries, or specification libraries, maintained by the company's quality organization, provide central sources of information. However, if you are going to be spending many months writing a book that must comply precisely to a customer or internal company specification, then you should have it at your fingertips. Otherwise, you will spend a lot of unproductive time walking back and forth to the central source.

Standards

Standards fall into two categories. There are industry and government standards that provide guidelines for text and graphics preparation. For example, the IEEE (Institute of Electrical and Electronic Engineers) standards on abbreviations and symbology are accepted standards across the country. Without them, the information used in a technical book may well be misunderstood. There are also company standards that must be complied with to meet local or customer requirements. Whichever are used, the writer should be familiar with them and have them readily available so that questions can be quickly resolved.

Statements of Work

Statements of work are part of a procurement contract that contain specific details concerning documentation requirements. For example, reviews, schedules, and even definitions may be found within a statement of work. It is important that the writer be thoroughly familiar with the statement of work and all established milestones so personal goals can be set to ensure compliance with all contractual commitments.

Where government contracts are involved, there is often a contract data requirements list (CDRL), sometimes called a DD Form 1423, that specifies deliverable materials, delivery dates, and other information that can have an impact on the publications production schedule. When this is the case, the writer should be sure to obtain a copy of the CDRL along with the statement of work to ensure his or her familiarity with all contractual obligations.

Style Guides

Style guides are often invaluable for quickly resolving questions related to style. For example, if there is a question about preferred words, the style guide should have the answer. An example of this may be in the area of action verbs in a book that contains procedural information. Are switches "set," "positioned," "rotated," "turned," or "pressed?" Do panel lamps "light" or "illuminate?" Do they "go out" or "extinguish?" How are illustrations referenced? Do the words "figure" and "chapter" begin with a capital letter or are they lowercased? All these questions can be answered with a good, authoritative style guide. This is particularly helpful when two or more writers may be writing portions of a large book and they need agreement on points of style. Both nationally accepted style guides, such as the University of Chicago's *A Manual of Style* or the *U.S. Government Printing Office Style Guide* can be used. In addition, company style guides are often available.

Samples

If you are about to write a technical book that describes a particular subject and the book must be prepared in accordance with a certain specification, there is no substitute for having a few sample books that have already been prepared on the same or similar subjects. If you happen to have a sample book that has been prepared in accordance with the same specification, you have hit the jackpot. This material will serve as a valuable model for your project. Instead of "reinventing the wheel," you simply begin "filling in the blanks."

When looking for samples, you might ask your customer, particularly if he or she is affiliated with the military or a large corporation, to loan you a sample. You will find that your customer is as eager as you are for you to do an accurate, fast-turnaround job.

USING VENDOR SERVICES

A number of good publications vendors around the country will be delighted to do work for you either "in-house,"that is, in their own facilities, or send subcontract people to your place of business. This is particularly true of technical writers and editors. Subcontractors also offer illustrating and photographic services, word processing and typesetting services, and even turnkey publishing services including printing. The following paragraphs provide some tips on dealing with vendor and freelance assistance.

Before describing the various publications services that are available, it is essential that subcontractors, particularly those who will be providing services in their own facility, have a clear understanding of what is needed. To do this, it is necessary to have a detailed statement of work which specifies precisely what you want done, what materials are to be used, major milestones including in-process and final reviews, and provisions for rework in the event that you are not satisfied with the product as submitted.

Bidder's conferences are often in order where your requirements are explained to a number of potential subcontractors at the same time. Each can be given a specification of the work to be performed. Once you have described the work and have answered all questions, the bidders return to their places of business, estimate the job, and, by knowing that they are competing head-on with other bidders, will most often give you an attractive price.

Writers and Editors

Whether the writer or editor is freelance or submitted by a reputable subcontract publications services house, you should screen all applicants as if you were going to hire them as permanent employees. They will be living with the project for the duration, and you had better make sure that they are qualified, and have the personal traits for which you are looking. They will be representing your organization when they interface with subject matter experts, and you will want to be represented in a professional manner. Remember, freelancers and vendors are anxious to make a sale and are sometimes optimistic in their claims about temporary help, whom they may barely know. Look at them hard, check with former employers, and in the case of technical writers, test their technical knowledge. Also try to determine how long you will be able to count on their help. Temporary employees have a tendency to pick up and move at the first sign of "greener pastures."

Many small companies or individual authors cannot afford the luxury of maintaining a full-time professional editor, who can perform an in-depth grammatical edit. If you happen to be writing a book for a major publisher, you will find that part of the publisher's function will be to provide both editing and proofreading services. However, if you are providing your work as a finished product, you may want the help of a freelance or subcontract editor. There are a number of editors available who will do a reasonably good job. Some charge by the hour, some by the page, and others by the job. Whatever the case, it is good to have the objectivity of an editor. They will be sympathetic to the reader's point of view, which is exactly what you are looking for.

Illustrators and Graphic Arts Personnel

Both of these categories, which include technical illustrators, advertising artists, and photographers, often look upon their field as art. Truly, the good ones are artists. As artists, you must treat them accordingly. Although they are usually not as expensive as writers, they take a great deal of pride in their work and are often sensitive to criticism; more so than the professional writer, who should know that he or she is being paid to provide what the customer thinks is good, not what the writer thinks is good. This may be part of the dilemma: writers are paid to tolerate criticism that sometimes approaches abuse; graphics people are not. Of course, the same careful screening process should be given to graphics people as is given to writers and editors. Although they are not required to interface with subject matter experts and clients as often, it is still important to ensure that they are fully qualified to perform the job, will get along with the work group, and plan to be around long enough to finish the project.

Word Processing and Typsetting Services

Often, companies use outside word processing and typesetting services, especially when their publications load is not heavy enough to justify economically employing the people and purchasing or leasing the equipment necessary to perform word processing or typesetting within the company.

Word Processing Services. Normally, writers who create their manuscript in longhand must have it draft typed to submit the manuscript to review. The review copy must be as legible as possible for several reasons. First, if the manuscript is difficult to read, the subject matter expert involved in the review will be inefficient. There is a tendency to wait until the copy is of reasonably good quality before making changes. Some reviewers seem to make more changes on typeset copy than on draft typed copy. In any case, it is necessary to give the reviewer a fully legible copy of the preliminary book to help ensure his or her doing the best job possible.

There are a number of sources of word processing services. These range from publications service companies to individual word processing operators who work in their homes. If your book is to be typeset, it may be more economical to find a full-service publications business that uses word processors as input devices for their typesetting equipment. In this way the book only has to be keyboarded one time. The time and expense associated with rekeyboarding for typesetting will be eliminated.

Typesetting Services. There are typesetting services available in almost every city. The systems used vary from "direct type," that is, typewriters that use a variety of type face styles and sizes, to sophisticated, high-speed photocomposers. Photocomposition is the most versatile typesetting method used today. Some systems have up to 40 different type styles available at any given time ranging in size from 0.075 inch to over 1 inch. They can output up to 3,000 lines of high-quality type per minute.

When using outside typesetters, it is good to shop the price. In addition to looking for the best price, you should always examine the quality of the typesetter's product. Look at recent samples to determine if the product will be satisfactory. Although most typesetters produce good-quality product, the developing process may be sloppy which will give you weak or poor contrast type on dingy paper.

In addition to looking at type quality, ensure that the paper used is suitable for long-term retention. One inexpensive photocomposition paper used is only good for a matter of days. If left in direct light, it can fade to the point of being completely unusable in a matter of hours. This material, called stabilization-base paper, is used primarily for newspapers where the camera-ready reproducible masters need only be kept for a day or two. The stabilization-base paper is ideal for this kind of application and saves the user material costs. Resin-coated paper lasts indefinitely, but it is more expensive.

Besides looking at price, quality, and the durability of the material used, you should also determine what typefaces are available. This includes both size and style. Be sure that the vendor has the capability to respond to your needs before you sign the contract. You may find that a vendor whose in-house capability is limited will have to subcontract some of the work. When this is the case, be sure that the second-tier subcontractor is reliable. You can find your schedule in jeopardy due to the inability of a second-tier vendor to respond to the primary-tier subcontractor's needs.

Printing Services

Once again, if you subcontract your production to a turnkey publications service company, printing may be part of the package offered. If printing is the only thing you require from an outside vendor, you will want to shop for a printer in the same way you selected a typesetter. Find one who can provide film work, platemaking, offset duplication, collating, and binding services.

As in typesetting, it is a good practice to avoid multiple-tier printing subcontractors. When examining a printer's quality, look at the darkness of the ink and the cleanliness of the paper and check the quality of halftones (printed photographs). Ensure that they are clear. Look at the dot pattern carefully. Is it an 85-line or a 133-line screen? Does the printer use screened prints or does he or she combine line and tone negatives? These techniques are described in Chapter 10. For now, it is sufficient to say that the quality of a printed page and a close look at printed photographs are good indicators of what you can expect from a printer.

TYPEWRITERS, WORD PROCESSORS, AND DICTATION EQUIPMENT

This section describes some of the tools used by writers to help them get their words on paper in the least amount of time. All these tools require some special skills, but these skills can normally be mastered in a matter of weeks, and at the most, a few months.

Typewriters

Today most professional writers can type. Some still use longhand, but the majority of writers realize the necessity for keyboard skills and type their own manuscripts. When using typewriters, the manuscripts are often "chock full" of strikeovers and painted with Liquid Paper. Blocks of text are often cut out with scissors and are relocated in the manuscript with tape. Although the manuscript is often too messy to use as a review copy, the typewriter helps the author to get words on paper quickly.

An author who can type between 40 and 60 words per minute produces a lot more work than does one struggling to produce 25 words a minute in longhand. Of course, if a manuscript is filled with corrections, it can be processed through a draft typing stage prior to being distributed for review.

Word Processors

Perhaps one of the most productive uses of a word processor is when it is used by a professional writer. Word processors have revolutionized the office, where secretaries and typists can produce four to five times more work in the same amount of time. The savings potential in an area where salaries are relatively low "pays back" the equipment investment in less than a year in many cases. Just think what can be gained in productivity and payback when equipping highly paid authors.

Word processing systems, like typewriters, require keyboard skills. In addition, some special training is required to familiarize an author with the various functions offered by the word processing equipment. Most writers can be productive on a word processing system in under two days. They may not know every feature available on the system, but the ability to insert, delete, move, copy, and print out letter-perfect text in a fraction of the time required on a standard typewriter makes word processing equipment for authors an attractive investment. In addition to offering an increase in author productivity, the need for draft typing is often eliminated.

Some businesses use their publications word processing systems to capture the keystrokes that will ultimately be used by their in-house typesetter. When this is done, an enormous production savings can be realized. There is one drawback, however. When a system is developed that couples word processors directly with typesetters, there is often the need to embed special typesetting codes in the text. These codes are instructions used by the typesetter to produce various paragraph-level headings, line spacing, type styles, and so on. When writers find themselves as concerned with the typesetting codes as they are with the words they are writing, they begin to slow down. It is a mistake to burden professional authors with typesetting. Professional writers should restrict their material to text only; typesetting operators should be available to convert the text into the proper form for the typesetter.

Dictation Equipment

Many writers use dictation equipment to collect information from subject matter experts. For example, the writer may prepare a list of questions, make an appointment with one of the source people, and capture the interview on tape. This eliminates the necessity to make handwritten notes. The subject matter expert can answer the questions in the time it takes to have a brief conversation, saving everyone a great deal of time.

I personally have done book research using a small pocket-sized tape recorder and have found it to be a powerful tool for collecting detailed information. If you happen to be writing a philosophical passage, you will find that people tend to talk more freely than they write. Their biases, emotions, and strong expressions of concern will be easily detected on audio tape. Additional information on tape recorder research is presented in Chapter 11.

If the subject matter expert appears to be nervous at the prospect of being recorded, tell him a joke, talk about the weather, or have a casual discussion about something of mutual interest while the recorder is running. Once he sees that it is harmless, he will most often forget that it is there and will begin talking freely.

When you get the tapes back to your desk, you can either give them to a draft typist for transcription or you can plug them into a transcriber and begin keyboarding the information yourself. The latter approach is usually the better, because you can make the sentences read correctly as you transcribe the recorded information. You will find that subject matter experts tend to ramble and repeat themselves even when they have an outline to follow. If you are fortunate enough to have a display-based word processor, you will find that you can quickly organize the material in the proper sequence and remove the redundant passages using the word processor's move and delete functions.

DRAWING TOOLS

Most books, especially those that must convey technical concepts, require illustrations. The illustrations fall into three general categories. These are line drawings (pictures made with lines), tone art (photographs that, when printed, are made up of varying dot densities to effect gray tones), and combination line and tone art. Obviously, drawing a straight line requires a straight edge or drafting triangle and a pencil or pen. Making uniform circles, boxes, diamonds, and other shapes requires various drawing templates. Symbols used on diagrams and schematics require special symbol templates. You should also obtain grid or graph paper to help you keep relative sizes and spacing consistent.

Review the kinds of illustrations you will be required to prepare. Of course, these will usually be sketches or concepts; professional illustrators will likely redraw these for final reproduction unless the book happens to be a low-budget project. In any case, it is important to make the illustrations as clear as possible in the least amount of time. This is where the drawing tools come in. They allow straight lines, round circles, and square boxes to be drawn, and they help even the most artistically inept writer to convey clearly the kind of shape or symbol needed.

Templates, triangles, and other drawing tools and supplies can be obtained from most well-stocked art or drafting supply stores. The phone book will likely list a number of them. Some large companies with drafting and art departments stock these tools as standard operating supplies or have provisions for employees to buy these tools and supplies at a negotiated discount.

Whatever the arrangement, be sure to make a list of the tools that you will need and obtain them before trying to sketch your illustrations. Believe me, it will make artwork preparation a much simpler and more satisfying task.

PERSONALITY

As a professional writer, your personality can be one of the most valuable tools in your bag of tricks, or it can be your downfall. A writer depends on others for information. This includes engineering, quality control, manufacturing, packing and shipping, design and drafting, library, and a number of other people who have vital information that you need for writing your book. If you charge your sources like a buffalo, you may never see them again; they will put you off and even hide from you if they can. Nobody likes to deal with offensive people.

If you are interviewing someone for technically detailed information and you disagree with what he or she is telling you, do not argue. Go away quietly and do a little more research. Then, if you are sure you are right, return and tactfully explain that you are not sure you understand the material completely. Never debate — all you will gain is alienation. Who knows, you may need inputs from this source again; if you turn the source off, he or she may stay turned off.

Technical writers should be pleasant to deal with from the subject matter expert's point of view. If they like you, they will gladly spend time with you. In fact, some will seek you out just to give you a hand. There are a number of ways to collect information. Several are described in Chapter 4.

Another important aspect of personality is the ability to get along with your colleagues in publications support functions. Draft typists, photocomposer operators, editors, illustrators, and other project writers are all important to the success of your job. You should be sensitive to your personal relationships with them. Be sure you consider their needs; you will need their help if you are to be successful. And if you want to hold a supervisory position, their opinion of you may make a difference.

THE "TEMPORARY EXPERT"

By definition, a good technical writer becomes a "temporary expert" in the subject area being described. As mentioned in Chapter 1, this is one of the rewards of the profession. It is a continuous education.

To be a good writer, you must be able to absorb a large volume of information in a relatively short time. After all, you cannot clearly describe anything to anyone, particularly if it is complicated, until you know all about it yourself. This means that you should make it a point to collect and study all pertinent material.

Become as knowledgeable about the subject as possible. If you do not, you will only be able to reproduce text that is "spoon fed" by your subject matter experts. Because subject matter experts are usually detailed technical people, they often assume that the reader already has a basic understanding of the involved principles. Not so! It is up to you, as a professional writer, to bring the objectivity needed to make the treatment clear to a reader who may not have any prior background in the subject area. This is a major responsibility of a good technical writer. Learn the subject as thoroughly as possible in the allotted time, anticipate the reader's unfamiliarity with it, and describe it so that he or she will understand it with relative ease.

REVIEW QUESTIONS

1. Why is it important for a writer to have access to current engineering change information?

2. What four documents serve as important tools to the technical writer?

3. Name two style guides that are in common use among technical writers.

4. How can sample books be used?

5. Name five types of subcontract services used for publications support.

6. Name some tools used by writers that help them put words on paper.

7. Why should a writer be equipped with basic drawing tools?

8. What is meant by the term *temporary expert*?

3 Organizing Your Work

INTRODUCTION

This chapter provides some tips on how to get your writing project started. You will find some ideas about developing a project file, pulling together your reference materials, becoming familiar with the subject matter, and gleaning existing materials to make your project easier.

BUILDING A PROJECT FILE

Most writing projects have numerous administrative and reference documents associated with them as well as a multitude of sketches, notes, contact names, phone numbers, and so on. The construction of a project file is an important records management task.

Develop a Filing System

First, ensure that you have a designated place in which to keep all your information. This can either be a file cabinet or desk drawer. Once the location is identified, make a list of the categories of information that you will be required to keep. Such a list might include the following entries:

1. Original cost estimate data
2. Actual cost data
3. Original scheduling information
4. Actual scheduling information
5. Contract, statement of work, specification, and style information

6. Sample materials (text, tables, illustrations, and other materials that can be used as samples for the current project)
7. Project contacts (names, addresses, and phone numbers of technical resource and production people)
8. Pertinent memorandums and telephone conference notes
9. Resource information (text and drawings organized by subject or chapter)

Physically Separate Material By Category

Each file should be separated by keeping it in a separate folder or three- ring binder. Two-hole fastener folders are also convenient. Contrary to normal practice, these are easier to use if the two-hole punch is made at the bottom of each sheet rather than at the top. This lets you thumb through the material without taking it out of the folder to see page titles, dates, or other heading information.

Develop a Master Index Sheet

It is often a good idea to keep a master index sheet in the front of each file that inventories the materials within. This will eliminate the need to search through the entire folder to see if the document you need is there. At a minimum, the master index sheet should contain a brief title and date of each document in the file. The file itself should be arranged in chronological order with the most recent date on top. If the contents of the file are numbered, it may be better to file the material by file number rather than by date.

Date and Initial All Material

You should date and initial every document in your file system. There are a number of reasons for this. First, it provides configuration control for you. If you have two documents in your file, neither of which is dated by the originator, you will be able to tell which was produced more recently.

Another reason is proof of receipt. There are times when it is important to verify to other people on the project which document is most current or precisely when a document was initiated or received. The only evidence may be the date and your initials. Get in the habit of dating and initialing all correspondence and other important information worthy of retention.

Maintain File System

Once you have built your filing system, maintain it. Do not let things pile up until it becomes a major chore to put everything away. Simply put things in their place when they are received. If you do, your file will always be ready for use, and you will not be faced with the dreaded job of going through a mountain of paperwork just to put your file in order.

There are times when writers have the good fortune of having clerical support. When this is the case, you may want to have a clerk maintain your file. However, do not just turn everything over to a file clerk or secretary. Be sure that you influence the organization of the file. You are the one who knows what is important and what is not. The items with the highest priority and usage should be the easiest to retrieve. Be sure that the file clerk understands the system and the reasons for retaining certain documents, and, by all means, arrange to have access to the file in the event the clerk is absent or if you need information outside normal working hours.

Maintain File Security

Whenever you store information containing cost estimates and schedules, there is a good chance that the information may contain sensitive data, considered proprietary to your company; or for that matter, it may be Department of Defense (DOD) classified information.

Company proprietary information must be under lock and key in a secure container. Every large company has procedures for safeguarding classified information. In the case of DOD classified documentation, there are established procedures for approving classified facilities, containers, and the personnel that handle that documentation. Be sure that these guidelines are thoroughly understood by every person who has access to the file. Further, be sure that unauthorized access to this kind of information is strictly forbidden. Only people who have the correct clearance level and a "need to know" should be authorized access to classified files.

Maintain Duplicate Files

There are times when files do not make a lot of sense. For example, if your department keeps a central file that you refer to infrequently, it may be more trouble than it is worth to develop a duplicate file of your own. You should evaluate the effort required to build your own private file against the effort involved in access to the central file. In addition to effort, you should also think through the impact on space. If space is at a premium, you may decide that you are not willing to pay the price in personal storage space to develop an extensive filing system of your own. On the other hand, if you have ample space and it is a half-block walk to the central file, you may decide a duplicate file of your own is worthwhile.

In the event that you decide not to develop your own file, but live out of the files of others, it is a good idea to develop a source list. This list should contain those documents that you need for reference, a brief description of their contents, and where they are available. In this way, you will know exactly what is available and where to go to get what you need. One precaution should be mentioned, however. You cannot always depend on other people to retain important documentation where it is readily retrievable unless you are assured that they have an established filing system of their own. If they do, you are probably in fairly good shape. If they do not, you should consider making copies of important documents for your own file.

PREVAILING SPECIFICATIONS AND GUIDELINES

There are many types of specifications and guidelines, and often a publications contract will involve a great many. For example, a single detail specification, which provides guidelines on subject matter content, specific treatments with examples, and audience, will normally list subordinate specifications. The subordinate specifications will cover such things as standard abbreviations, standard symbols used on illustrations, style and format conventions, preparation of camera-ready reproducible copy, preparation of photolithographic negatives, and much more.

Review the Specifications Before You Start

You should review prevailing specifications and guidelines before starting the actual writing process. Even when you are part of an organization having a dedicated publications production group, you **cannot** depend entirely on others to attend to page layout and paragraph or illustration numbering. In the long run, it will be cost effective for you to familiarize yourself with specified format and style. Then, you can develop a manuscript that adheres to the general format requirements, which will make life much easier for the editing staff.

Interpret the Specifications

Specifications are normally the standard used to measure the publications product. Detail and subordinate specifications cover every aspect of the publication. Where specifications stop, contracts, contract exhibits, and statements of work continue. These documents identify schedules and major milestones and often state who the final authority is in matters of interpretation.

Because many specifications are ambiguous, either by wording or omission of data, it is vital to identify the final authority and, next, to obtain interpretations and examples to resolve key questions. Once you know what the customer is looking for, you can proceed with relatively good assurance that what you are doing is right.

Often, the detail specification states that it is the final word in all matters of interpretation. When this is the case, ambiguities between a detail specification and a general specification can be resolved. In addition, when ambiguities exist between a passage of text and an illustration within a specification, the text prevails.

FAMILIARIZATION
WITH THE SUBJECT MATTER

Knowing what the book is supposed to look like is one thing; it is entirely another matter to know what is supposed to be in it. If you are writing about a specific technology, it is always good to have background that will help you understand the subject matter sufficiently to describe it. If not, you have got to get busy learning everything you can about the subject matter.

Reference Material

One of the first places you will want to start is in the area where the technology is in use. For example, if you are going to describe an electric toaster or an airborne radar system, see what it looks like inside and out. Talk to the technical people about it. Get drawings and specifications. If available, get reference books that describe the technology so you will be able to develop the proper vocabulary to discuss the product with the design people.

Look at the parts; watch the assembly process. Determine what functions the controls perform, and if possible, watch the product in action. You will not only learn about what it is and what it does, you will find that knowing about it makes the job easier, more interesting, and even fun. You will feel as if you are a part of the team that is bringing the product to market — and by the way, you are!

Reviewing Similar Projects

Among the best sources of information available are publications on similar products, particularly if they have been written to the same specification. Even if the product is drastically different, the book itself will serve as an excellent model for the pending publication project. If the specification is the same, the organization will be parallel. Illustrations and tables will exist; you will be able to take these and "fill in the blanks" with your own information. If you do not have any books at your location, call the customer and see if he or she can send you an example. This is actually far better than having one of your own, because the firm will send you one it likes. When this is the case, you will have a model that has been approved by the customer and that will resolve a variety of questions. Of course, be sure to tell the customer you are looking for an example of a book with which he or she is satisfied. This will let the customer know that you are going to model the new book after the one the firm sends you.

By simply looking, asking questions, and collecting and studying written information and drawings, you will become extremely familiar with the subject matter in a minimum amount of time. And when you finish the project, you will be an expert.

Often, the technical writer serves as a technical consultant when customers have questions about a product. This is particularly true of systems that have many elements. Engineers who are concerned with a specific piece often have no idea as to what is beyond their "black box." They simply do not have a system orientation.

I have been involved in situations where system-level customer inquiries were referred to me, the project technical writer, because no one else was available to answer system-level technical questions. At first, I found myself feeling unqualified to deal with the technical questions, but then, much to my surprise, I discovered that I had become an expert. There I was, fielding detailed technical questions and firing back detailed technical answers with little difficulty. After all, it was all in the book I had been working on, and I had to understand the subject matter before I could write about it.

REVIEW QUESTIONS

1. What containers are typically used to maintain project files?

2. What categories of information are kept in a project file?

3. What is a *master index sheet*?

4. Give reasons for dating and initialling filed material.

5. When should material be filed?

6. What is meant by the phrase *need to know*?

7. What is a *source list*?

8. Explain why it is important to know which contract document has precedence (or final authority)?

9. What are two general areas for obtaining project guidance?

10. How can a writer help to satisfy customer inquiries?

4

Project
Research

INTRODUCTION

This chapter describes the research process. Although project research is not a direct management tool, it can represent up to 70 percent of a writer's time. Therefore, some suggestions are included to help writing project managers structure their writing team's data collection techniques.

Experienced writers understand that the research phase of a project is extremely important in at least two areas. First, the fruits of research should yield accurate, pertinent information. Second, the writer must develop and use efficient collection techniques. The types of information that are normally available, collection techniques, and the compilation process are all addressed in this chapter.

RESEARCH TIME
VERSUS WRITING TIME

When considering a writing project, many inexperienced writers assume that most time is spent forming words and putting them on paper. However, depending on the subject matter, the time required to research a project can take well over half the total time spent by a writer. For example, if the book is being written about an extremely complex technical subject, and the writer is required to "dig out" the material from available technical design documentation, the ratio of research time to writing time could be 3 or 4 to 1.

If, on the other hand, a writer is simply reformatting readily available documentation or is writing relatively simple overview material, the research-to-writing ratio could be in the neighborhood of 1 to 3 or 4. The ratio of writing time to research time must be considered during the cost estimating, budgeting, and scheduling phases of a writing project. If the complexity is not considered, the result can be an overrun in time and money.

QUALITY OF AVAILABLE SOURCE MATERIAL

One of the determinants of research to writing time is the level, or quality, of available source material. Another is the proximity of the source material to the writer's work location. In the following paragraphs, source material input levels and availability are discussed.

Proximity of Source Material to the Writer's Work Location

Many experienced writing group supervisors will tell you that the only way to do a good job of gathering up-to-date information is physically to locate the writer with the information source. This does a number of things. It eliminates the time necessary to travel from a remote work area to the source area. It helps to establish an *esprit de corps* by having the writer coupled directly to the project on which he or she is working. The writer becomes "one of the gang" by working, eating, and perhaps car pooling with the project engineering people.

This makes it easier, more natural, and practical for the technical staff to provide the writer with timely information about finished designs or modifications. In some companies, writers are often part of the engineering organization rather than part of a central writing or publications organization. This is advantageous from a belonging point of view, but it sometimes has drawbacks when the writer must be measured against a room full of design engineers when it is time to divvy up the raise money. For this reason, larger companies usually maintain a central publications organization to which writers report. This allows them to be measured against one another based on their performance as writers, rather than as engineers.

Occasionally, a writer who is working away from the central publications and writing organization can experience some minor disadvantages. Failure to receive information about the latest style changes, or for that matter, having input to their formulation, can be a slight disadvantage and even cause some minor rework. But the importance of efficient source collection normally outweighs the inconveniences.

Raw Engineering Source Data

When a writer is technically oriented, he or she may be able to collect raw engineering data, such as product specifications, computer listings, design drawings, and photographs and decipher the information into a clearly written, easily understood publication. On the other hand, if a writer is not technically oriented, it may be necessary to spend a considerable amount of time interviewing design and maintenance engineers. Even when questions are answered, it is possible that the nontechnical writer will not absorb enough information to do a satisfactory job. Descriptions may result in vague attempts at technical descriptions. The key to this level of input, then, is ensuring that the writer assigned to the project has enough background in the subject area to make use of raw engineering source data.

Written Manuscripts and Transcriptions

Another common source of information is written manuscripts, either in handwriting or transcribed from dictation, that is provided by designated technical people in the project engineering and maintenance areas. When source material is to be obtained in this form, be certain that those preparing the material are thoroughly familiar with what is needed. Provide them with an annotated copy of the publications specification and an outline of the book. Discuss the requirements until you are satisfied that they have a clear understanding of the requirements. If left to his or her own devices, an innovative engineer will likely design an entire publications philosophy. Well meaning and meritorious as it may be, it will likely miss the mark.

It can be embarrassing, not to mention a waste of valuable time and money, to have to go back to the technical staff and ask them to do it again, only the right way this time. These people are not professional writers. Most do not like to write. And when they do, you will find that most have a severe case of "pride of authorship." Asking them to do it over is often perceived as personal insult. Even when this is not the case, most will be too busy to prepare their inputs a second time — so do everything possible to make it right the first time.

Typed Draft

There are times when the engineering staff does perform the writing job. This is typical in small companies that cannot afford the luxury of a full- time technical writing staff or that lack sufficient funds to subcontract the publications work. The result is often a typed draft. The draft is normally fed to an editor, who does a summary rewrite job, puts the material in the approved format, arranges illustrations, and then either passes it on to publications production or coordinates the production phase personally.

Although the small company may believe this to be the most cost effective approach to developing its product manuals, it is possibly the most expensive. Of course, if the engineering staff is not busy with new product development, then it may be a sound approach. If, on the other hand, there is a shortage of good design people available, you will probably find a design staff that is doing a poor job in both documentation and design. The company winds up with poor product documentation, resulting in user frustration, poor company image, and haphazard design work on following projects staffed by engineers who are trying to be "Jacks of all trades."

SOURCE COLLECTION TECHNIQUES

A number of strategies exist for collecting source material; these vary depending on the technical detail and the volume of information required. In the following paragraphs, strategies for source collection are described, including

- Multiple-source strategies
- Source collection through readily available documentation
- Source collection through personal interviews
- Dictation equipment
- Data collection packages

Multiple-Source Strategies

Because areas of a book project vary in size and complexity, it is necessary to have different source collection strategies for different kinds of information. To help decide how material will be gathered, it may be a good idea to draft an outline of the book containing the source method for each major section of the book. Once this is done, you can begin developing the tools needed to collect information for each area. Let us look at some of these collection methods.

Source Collection through Readily Available Documentation

Often many available documents can serve as resource material for publications development. These include such things as existing books on the same or similar subjects and contractually required documents such as product specifications and engineering drawings.

These documents should be screened and, wherever possible, used as background documents when writing descriptive material of a general nature. Of course, this kind of information is rarely directly applicable when writing specific technical descriptions or maintenance procedures. It can, however, be used as a basis for format and style. This is particularly true of existing books written on similar subject matter for the same or similar users. If the existing book was not well accepted by the users, it may be a good idea to analyze what areas are considered poor and find the right approach to presentation.

Source Collection through Personal Interviews

Once an outline is prepared and the subject matter experts are identified, it is often cost effective to schedule question and answer sessions with the subject matter experts. To be meaningful, you should schedule the sessions in advance and provide the subject matter expert with a list of questions or an outline of the section that you will be discussing. To make the most of the session, be sure that your list of questions is thorough.

When the interview starts, be sure to take careful notes. Also, obtain copies of sketches or any documents that may be pertinent or used as reference by the subject matter expert. Time limitations often require that the session be as efficient as possible. Do not spend a lot of time making small talk; some may be necessary to establish a good working relationship, but your time and the time for the subject matter expert is valuable, so do not waste it.

It is often efficient to use a tape recorder during a subject matter expert interview. The next section describes the use of a tape recorder in the source collection process and provides some tips on do's and don'ts.

Dictation Equipment

Using dictation equipment in subject matter expert interviews can be extremely efficient if you make the proper preparation and use the resulting tapes in an efficient manner. Let us take a look at a few practices that may be helpful.

The Interview. The interview should be scheduled in advance, just as any interview. The subject matter expert should be given an outline of the material to be covered in advance to allow adequate preparation. Before you begin the interview, you should explain to the subject matter expert that it will be helpful if he or she mentions the title of each topic as it is discussed so that you will know exactly where you are when the interview is being transcribed.

Once the interview starts, turn the tape recorder on and have a brief conversation, even small talk, to put the subject matter expert at ease. If he or she sees you talking freely with the recorder running, the expert will understand that your interview will be in the conversational mode rather than a structured report. This tends to put the interviewee expert at ease. Finally, if you have a small recorder, such as a microcassette unit that is barely noticeable, the subject matter expert will be more likely to forget its presence. If you have a large, imposing unit, the subject matter expert may become more occupied with the recorder than with the discussion.

Interact in the discussion. Ask questions; make observations. This will help to draw the subject matter expert into the content and away from the tape recorder. In addition, it will ensure that you have covered those items that you require for your book. Sometimes, it is good to keep a set of notes in parallel with the recorder. This serves two purposes. It lets the subject matter expert know that you are listening and keeps him or her focused on you as the audience. It also gives you the opportunity to write down questions to be answered when the time is right. If you interrupt the discussion to ask the question, you will find that some people will lose their direction, and you may miss important inputs.

Conversational inputs tend to be redundant. You will become aware of the same material being described two or three times. Do not interrupt; let them say it again — they may add a new dimension. You can carve out the redundancy during the transcription process.

One final thought about taped interviews. Be sure to number every tape and maintain a log showing subject matter, tape number, and interviewee. Then, when you return to your office, you will be able to organize the tapes and know exactly which ones address what subject. If they go unnumbered, not only do you run the risk of having to find information by searching through hours of tape but you may wind up recording over a valuable interview.

The Transcription Process.   Once you have returned to your office with the tapes, it is time to begin transcribing the discussions to paper. If you type, particularly on word processing equipment, and if you have a transcription machine, it will be much more efficient if you transcribe the material personally.

There are several reasons for this. The volume of information will be greatly shrunk. You will tend to eliminate and consolidate redundancy. You will let unrelated passages, such as small talk, go by without typing them. And you will edit the first-pass transcription into a readable draft rather than a rough manuscript requiring hours of typing and editing.

Many people do not verbalize complete sentences. They trail off; they run on; they use poor grammar; they break all the rules. So by transcribing the interviews yourself, the material will be much closer to final draft form than if you have a nonwriter do the transcription job.

Data Collection Packages

The use of data collection packages might be considered as an alternative to source collection. A data collection package (DCP) is a stylized, "fill- in-the-blanks" handout that can be used by subject matter experts as a guide to providing information.

Data Collection Package Applications. The best time to use DCPs is when your subject matter experts are unavailable or are many miles away. In either case, the DCP allows them to review what is required and fill in the necessary information. It is always a good idea to include contact information to enable the experts to resolve questions about what is needed by telephone or telegram.

When subject matter experts are pressed for time, the data collection package often allows them to provide their inputs when they find a convenient time, such as when a piece of lab equipment is undergoing preventive maintenance or repair. Since this kind of event is rarely scheduled, the expert may be able to squeeze in some unplanned time. The alternative, which is to schedule a personal interview, may never be convenient.

Data Collection Package Content. The content of a DCP includes the following information:

1. Cover sheet describing DCP use, schedule, and contact information.
2. Contents sheet listing each section of the DCP.
3. Excerpts from DCPs showing typical responses, writing style, sketches, and any other pertinent input guidelines.
4. Sections for each subject to be covered.

5. An outline at the beginning of each section. Where helpful, sample write-ups and sketches should be included to ensure that the subject matter expert has a clear understanding of what is required.
6. Ample blank pages in each section for write-ups and sketches. Graph paper can be supplied to encourage drawings.
7. A list of specifications or other helpful documents to encourage the subject matter expert to supply copies.

The main element of a DCP is convenience. If it is not clear and easy to use, the subject matter expert probably will not use it. In my many years of data collection, I have found mixed response. Some source people enjoyed using them and provided an abundance of excellent information, making the writing job a literal "snap." Others, who perhaps do not like to write things on paper or do not have their schedules under control, require extensive follow-up. Some have failed miserably. When this is the case, you will have to resort to an alternate source collection method.

THE COMPILATION PROCESS

As source material is collected, it should be cataloged and filed. You should begin the cataloging process as soon as the project is started rather than wait until you have a large collection of random data. The most common approach is to develop a filing system where source material is sorted by subject matter and book location. File folders or a notebook, depending upon the size of the project, can be used to store the materials.

It is always helpful to have a detail-level outline at the front of each storage location. Having an outline for each section lets you check off what has been received and what is still needed. In addition to knowing what is finished and what is needed, you can annotate the section outlines with source and scheduling information. This provides you with a detailed status of each section and with visibility as to what is required to complete the source effort.

When sufficient source material is available to begin writing the section, written manuscript can also be kept in the sections. If the project is small, you may wish to keep the manuscript with the source material. If it is large, you may wish to separate manuscript and source material into two parallel files.

As long as the project is active, it is advisable to keep the source material as a history file. This can be valuable during the review process, when you may be required to query one of your source files to verify information accuracy.

SUMMARY

The research process is a writer's bridge to success. Depending on the complexity of the material, the research phase often represents well over half the total project cost. Because it is a major cost factor, it is imperative that professional writers develop efficient techniques for gathering and filing their source information. There must be a workable strategy tied to a schedule and an organized compilation process. Above all, the writer must never lose sight of the fact that tact and diplomacy are vital tools, particularly when personal contact with subject matter experts is required.

REVIEW QUESTIONS

1. How does research time compare with writing time?

2. What are two factors affecting research time?

3. What are some problems associated with writing assignments within the engineering staff?

4. How can an existing publication serve as source material?

5. What list should a writer have when conducting a subject matter expert interview?

6. When using dictation equipment, what other tool should be used?

7. What information should a dictation interview log contain?

8. What is a *data collection package*?

9. What is the most important element of a data collection package to make it successful?

10. What tool can be used to record what source information has been received and what source information is still needed?

5

Cost Estimating

INTRODUCTION

It has been said that cost estimating is part of a game called "You Bet Your Business," and if your cost estimating is sloppy, you can be a big loser. A poor cost estimate can mean project overruns and a loss of profit. So, if your company is going to make a profit, it is necessary to prepare accurate cost estimates and include provisions for contingencies. There is always a level of risk associated with any cost estimate. When the risk is high, the price must reflect it. If the project is "a piece of cake," you can sell it for a lot less. The important thing is that you sell it for more than it costs you. This chapter discusses cost estimating in detail. It may be the most valuable chapter in the book as it provides a step-by-step cost-estimating process.

THE COST ESTIMATOR

Cost estimating is something that is usually assigned to senior-level, experienced writers. Some companies even have specialists in publications cost estimating. Why should cost estimators be senior? To do a good job of cost estimating, it is necessary to understand the scope of the effort. This means knowing the prevailing specifications, the difficulty of the technology involved, the availability of good source material, production processes and costs, risks, and the financial impact of quality control and provisions for customer reviews. In fact, just knowing the customer helps in doing a better job of cost estimating. Each customer is different. Some are easy to please, others are difficult. It is a matter of personality, and an experienced estimator will have case histories as background for judgment.

COST-ESTIMATING MULTIPLIERS

Before a reasonably accurate cost estimate can be made, it is important to develop a set of accurate cost multipliers. These multipliers should be based on standard costs, which are acquired by monitoring actual project costs over a sample period of time. The longer the sample period, the better the multipliers are likely to be.

The cost multipliers should include "windage" for complexity of the subject matter, access to source material, number of reviews, the arbitrary nature of the customer, the status of the product being described (risk of rework due to design changes), and other factors that can influence the cost of a project.

Once you know how many hours it should take to write a page of text, a table, or sketch an illustration; to edit these pages; to draft type them; to typeset them; to prepare the final artwork; and all the other tasks associated with the project, you are ready to develop a cost multiplier table. The table has two dimensions: production units and tasks. Table 5-1 contains an example of a publications cost multiplier table.

COST-ESTIMATING RATES

In addition to knowing how much time it takes to produce each publications unit, it is necessary to know the pay rates for each category of labor. Pay rates and material, travel, overhead, and profit are described in the following paragraphs. Table 5-2 contains a sample rate schedule that could be used in conjunction with the publications cost multiplier table.

The rates used are normally based on the average wages of a job classification. When a known senior or junior resource is being used, adjustments can be made accordingly. Notice

TABLE 5-1   A Standard Publications Cost Multiplier Table

| Task | PRODUCTION UNIT | | | | | |
| | Text | | Line Art | | Tone Art | |
	Text	Tab	Full	Part	Full	Part
Research and write	4.0	5.0	4.0	2.0	2.0	2.0
Edit	0.3	0.4	0.2	0.1	0.1	0.1
Production edit	0.2	0.2	0.2	0.1	0.2	0.2
Draft type	0.3	0.6	0.1	0.05	0.05	0.05
Typeset	0.5	0.8	0.3	0.2	0.05	0.05
Proofread	0.3	0.4	0.2	0.1	0.05	0.05
Illustrate	0.0	0.0	6.0	3.0	3.0	1.5
Paste up	0.5	0.6	0.3	0.15	0.2	0.1

Litho, print, collate, and bind:

Positives, line/screen	0.15	0.15	0.1	0.1	0.15	0.15
Negatives, line/tone	0.25	0.25	0.25	0.15	0.3	0.25
Stripping, line/tone	0.15	0.15	0.15	0.15	0.2	0.15
Metal plates	0.08 per plate					
Processor plates	0.05 per plate					
Press time	0.1 per 1st 100 impressions; plus 0.03 per additional 100					
Collate	0.2 per 1,000 sheets					
Side stitch	1.0 per 1,000 sets					
Corner stitch	1.0 per 1,000 sets					
Saddle stitch	0.8 per 1,000 sets					
Three-hole drill	3.5 per 1,000 sets					
Perfect bind	1.7 per 1,000 sets					
Case bind	8.0 per 1,000 sets					

Change the total writing time by the amount indicated:

Writing Complexity Scale		Writing Source Quality Scale	
Simple	x 0.6	Outstanding	x 0.7
Below average	x 0.8	Excellent	x 0.85
Average	x 1.0	Satisfactory	x 1.0
Complex	x 1.5	Marginal	x 1.5
Extremely complex	x 2.0	Unsatisfactory	x 2.0

Notes:

In-process reviews	Add 6.0% to total writer time per review.
Postproduction reviews	Add 10% to all categories for first review. Add 5% to all categories for second review.
Administrative time	Add 5% to total writer time for project administration.

that multiplier and rate tables are marked "Company Classified Information." This means that only those people within the company who need access to perform their job are given this information. If this information falls into the hands of competitors, their ability to undercut bids increases significantly. In addition, disclosure of specific, sensitive departmental rates can create strife within an organization.

Other Costs

Aside from standard multipliers, labor rates, and page counts, there are other costs that we must comprehend in our estimate. These include

1. Material cost
2. Travel

TABLE 5-2 Publications Cost Estimating Rate Schedule

Effective January 1, 1985
(Company Classified Information)

Writer	$14.23	Proofreader	$6.95
Editor	13.18	Paste-up technician	8.76
Production editor	12.76	Litho technician	10.15
Draft typist	5.90	Press operator	8.85
Typesetter	8.54	Bindery operator	7.96
Illustrator	9.20		

3. Labor overhead
4. Material overhead
5. General and administrative costs
6. Profit (or fees)

These costs are added to the labor costs to determine the total cost of producing a publication. Let us briefly look at each of these costs.

Material. Material includes such items as special binders, subcontractor costs for such things as cover design, photography, printing, or any other service not normally done "in house."

Travel. Travel is the cost of trips that must be specifically made in the performance of a publication's preparation. Trips to the customer's facility for in-process reviews, trips to gather information necessary in writing the book, and other travel directly associated with the project may be added to the cost estimate.

To estimate travel costs, some companies use standard rates. For example, a two-day, one-night trip to the coast: $560.00. However, to be more accurate, you can prepare a travel estimate by checking air fare rates, motel rates, car rental rates, and budget a fixed amount for meals and tips. A schedule similar to the one following can be used for estimating travel expenses.

```
Air fare                                              $_____
Motel _____ days x $_____/day                         $_____
Meals _____ days x $_____/day                         $_____
Ground transportation:
Auto rental _____ days x $____/day (incl mileage)$_____
Storage and parking _____ days $____/day              $_____
Tips _____ days x $____/day                           $_____
Miscellaneous _____ days x $_____/day                 $_____
International airport taxes                            $_____
    Total travel                                      $_____
```

Labor Overhead. Labor overhead is a markup rate applied to direct labor. Overhead normally includes the administrative burden of employment, such as utilities, employee benefits, equipment and facilities depreciation, office supplies, and all other expenses associated with employing direct labor personnel. The labor overhead rate can be anywhere from 30 to 150 percent, depending on the company, facility, benefits, and many other factors involved. Obviously, the higher the overhead rate, the less competitive the price will be, so it is incumbent on management to control overhead levels.

Material Overhead. Material normally carries with it a slight overhead charge for the administrative time, paperwork associated with procurement and payment, and handling and storage.

General and Administrative Expenses. These are normally expenses associated with corporate administration. They include such things as personnel administration expenses, corporate security, corporate officers' salaries, and all other costs associated with maintaining a corporate entity.

Profit (or Fees). The profit or fee is what the company keeps as a reward for conducting business. It normally ranges from 8 to 20 percent, depending on the risk, the customer's willingness to pay, the competitive edge, and a number of other factors. Profit levels are often settled upon in final contract negotiations.

Let us look at these elements of cost in the following example.

Direct labor	$1,000.00
Labor overhead @ 80%	800.00
Material	250.00
Material overhead @ 10%	25.00
Subtotal	$2,075.00

```
General and Administrative
                @ 20%           415.00
        Subtotal              $2,490.00
     Profit @ 15%                373.50
     Total price             $2,863.50
                             ==========
```

ESTIMATING PAGES
AND ILLUSTRATIONS

Once approved cost multipliers and rates are established, the next task, and perhaps the most rigorous, is to estimate the number and type of pages to be contained in a publication. There are two variables that impact the number of pages. These are (1) the depth of coverage required and (2) the complexity of the subject matter. Let us look first at the depth of coverage.

Depth of Coverage

The depth of coverage is fixed by the governing specification. It will prescribe how much detail is required in a book, what kind of tables to provide, and the kind of illustrations needed. In the case of a technical manual to be used for operation and maintenance of a product, it is first necessary to understand the maintenance philosophy. Questions such as these must be answered:

1. Is the product repairable?
2. If repairable, who repairs it?
3. Can the operator make minor repairs where it is used?
4. Can a service technician repair it where it is used?
5. Can defective subassemblies be swapped out where it is used?
6. Should the entire unit be swapped out and returned to a repair center?

7. Should the user simply return it for repair?
8. Can the user trade it for an operating unit at a distributor facility?

Once these kinds of questions are answered, the publications cost estimator has a much better idea about the kind of coverage that will be required when the book is written. The product descriptions, technical details, maintenance procedures, accompanying diagrams, part lists, and all the other information that makes the book useful to the user or service technician can be determined. We will consider a typical example of how this information is used after we look at the impact of subject matter complexity.

Subject Matter Complexity

The complexity of the product being described by a publication obviously has a great deal to do with the size of the book. If you are describing the operation and maintenance of a can opener, even if you get into complete overhaul procedures, the book is not going to be very large. However, a field repair manual on something like an aircraft engine or radar system is going to be big. It is not enough to stand in front of the thing to be described and think big or little. You must tear into its innards, count and catalog the pieces, and determine how much information each piece will require to be adequately described. A large system can be like eating an elephant: you have to do it a bite at a time. Questions such as the following are used to determine the complexity of the subject matter:

1. How many major units of equipment are there?
2. How many subassemblies are there?
3. How many are simple mechanical?
4. How many are complex mechanical?
5. How many are simple electrical?
6. How many are complex electrical?

7. How many circuit boards are there?
8. How many single-sided circuit boards are there?
9. How many double-sided circuit boards are there?
10. How many discrete piece-parts are there for each subassembly?
11. How many rack or chassis-mounted piece parts are there?
12. How many operator control and indicator panels are there?
13. How many modes of operation exist?
14. How many cables and wiring harnesses exist?
15. How many service control and indicator panels exist?
16. How many special diagnostic or service procedures are there?

If the subject matter happens to be a digital computer system software system reference manual, the questions might include such things as

1. How many program utilities?
2. How many commands?
3. How many menus?
4. How many prompts?
5. How many and what type of input devices?
6. How many and what type of output devices?
7. How many output displays?
8. How many list types and formats?
9. How many error messages?

Depending on the product being described, additional or a considerably different set of questions might be appropriate. The key is to have a catalog of information that defines the subject matter to the extent that the cost estimator knows everything that must be described. Now that we have looked at the concept of depth of coverage and subject matter complexity, let us estimate the number of pages and illustrations in a technical book.

ESTIMATING THE SIZE OF A BOOK

Remember, before we can estimate the size of a book, we have to know what we are going to say about the subject (depth of coverage), and how complicated it is (complexity of subject matter). The following discussion summarizes the specification we are using. Then, the maintenance philosophy is described. Finally, the product complexity is defined.

Specification

The specification used is a company's "Best Commercial Practices," which references industry standards for such things as abbreviations and graphic symbols and company standards for page layout and type style. The outline for maintenance manuals is

Cover Page
Table of Contents
List of Illustrations
List of Tables
Chapter 1　General Description
Chapter 2　Installation
Chapter 3　Operating Instructions
Chapter 4　Theory of Operation
Chapter 5　Maintenance Procedures
Chapter 6　Parts List
Chapter 7　Diagrams
Appendices

The specification calls for the following major paragraphs within each of the chapters:

General Description
　　Purpose and Organization of the Book
　　Product Description
　　Capabilities and Limitations
　　Technical Characteristics

Installation
　　Introduction

Preparation for Installation
Unpacking
Equipment Setup
Postinstallation Checkout

Operating Instructions
Introduction
Operating Controls and Indicators
Turn-on Procedure
Turn-off Procedure
Normal Operating Procedures
Emergency Operating Procedures

Theory of Operation
Introduction
Overall Functional Description
Detailed Functional Descriptions

Maintenance Procedures
Introduction
Tools and Special Test Equipment
Operator-Level Maintenance
Preventive Maintenance Procedures
Cleaning and Inspection
Lubrication
Minimum Performance Standards
Corrective Maintenance Procedures
Fault Isolation
Disassembly Procedures
Reassembly Procedures

Parts List
Introduction
Parts Information

Diagrams
Introduction
Types of Diagrams
Special Terms and Symbols
Diagrams

The outline of the specification is not enough to do a thorough job. We also need to see what kind of illustrations and tables are used. A good specification contains many examples that provide guidance relative to the type of illustrations and tables to be used. This is helpful to the cost estimator as he or she will know how complicated the illustrations and tables will be. There are cases where oversized illustrations are used. These are called "foldout" illustrations and are often included in cost estimating schedules. However, everything is normally measured in standard page units. An 11" × 17" foldout is equivalent to two 8½" × 11" illustrations for cost-estimating purposes.

Maintenance Philosophy

Now that the specification has been described, it is time to determine the maintenance philosophy. In this example, we will assume that there are some operator maintenance items, such as changing fuses, panel lamps, and cleaning. Additional maintenance will be performed at the site of use by a qualified service technician.

The technician will be equipped with all necessary service tools and a set of plug-in replaceable subassemblies. When a defective unit is reported, the service technician will make a service call and simply swap out plug-in modules to repair the product. If the defect is a chassis-mounted part, a "loaner" unit will be left with the customer, and the defective unit will be taken to the service center for repair.

One addition twist is provided by the product marketing department. All user operation and maintenance procedures will be collected in a separate booklet for product customers. Distribution of the complete operation and maintenance manual will be restricted to service technicians.

Once we know how the product will be serviced, we can proceed to the next step: defining the complexity of the equipment.

Equipment Complexity

The product for which the book will be prepared is a television decoder unit. The product is supplied to pay TV subscribers. This unit is connected to antenna terminals of a TV set, and the TV antenna is then connected to a set of terminals on the converter unit. The unit has a standard power cord that can be connected to any standard AC power outlet. The front panel of the unit contains a power switch, a selector switch that allows the user to select any desired channel, and a set of 10 decoder switches. Scrambled transmissions from pay TV stations are decoded by the converter to allow subscribers to view any TV channel in a normal fashion. Decoding sequences are selectable by setting the decoder switches to prescribed positions. The decoder switch positions are supplied to subscribers on a monthly basis.

The unit contains a front panel with operating controls, two internal double-sided printed circuit cards, and one single-sided card. The double- sided cards contain approximately 85 piece parts each. The single-sided card contains 40 parts. The cover is removed by unscrewing eight screws. Front- panel parts are connected to the circuit cards by means of three quick- disconnect wiring harnesses. This allows the service technician to replace switches and lamps in the field. The circuit cards are interconnected by means of a wiring harness. The wiring harness can also be replaced in the field.

Functionally, the decoder unit has three major electronic circuits. First, there is a power supply circuit that converts AC power to DC voltage levels used by the unit. A signal processing circuit receives incoming television signals and inputs them to the decoder circuit. The decoder circuit unscrambles coded television signals and outputs them to the TV set's antenna terminals in a form suitable for input to a standard TV receiver.

Each subscriber will receive an operation and maintenance booklet with the unit. The operation section will describe turn-on, turn-off, channel selection, and special switch settings for viewing premium pay events such as title boxing matches. Maintenance procedures will include checking the power connection, a line fuse, and antenna terminal connections in the event of an operating problem. If these checks do not remedy the problem, a list of service centers and phone numbers is provided.

DEVELOPING THE PAGE
AND ILLUSTRATION COUNT

Now that we have a good description of the specification, the maintenance philosophy, and the product complexity, let us put it all together and develop a page and illustration count.

Using an Estimating Matrix

To keep track of everything, it is a good idea to develop an estimating matrix containing content outlines and page and illustration counts. Such an outline is provided in Table 5-3. Notice that both the service person's operation and maintenance manual and the user's booklet are contained in the table. Text pages, tabular pages, and illustration pages are all calculated by the cost estimator. The estimator must calculate the amount of text, tabular material, and illustration material based on the maintenance philosophy, the level of detail required, the specific product configuration, and to a large extent, personal experience as to what it takes to provide adequate coverage. In addition, the estimator may use existing books based on similar specifications and equipment for guidance.

The page counts are estimated by visualizing the amount of text, tabular, and illustration material associated with each component part of the subject matter. For example, each functional section is covered by text in the theory of operation chapter, each panel with operator's controls and indicators is

TABLE 5-3 A Cost Estimating Matrix used to Determine Page Counts

Description	PAGE UNITS		LINE ART		TONE ART		Totals
	Text	Tab	Full	Part	Full	Part	
Service manual							
Front matter	1.0	6.0	1.0				8.0
General description							
Purpose and Organization	0.5						0.5
Product description	1.5					1.0	2.5
Capabilities and limitations	1.0						1.0
Technical Characteristics	0.5	1.0					1.5
Subtotal	3.5	1.0	1.0			1.0	13.5
Installation							
Introduction	0.5						0.5
Preparation for Installation	1.0		1.0				2.0
Unpacking	0.5						0.5
Equipment setup	1.0		1.0				2.0
Postinstallation Checkout	1.5		1.0				2.5
Subtotal	4.5		3.0				7.5

Description	PAGE UNITS		LINE ART		TONE ART		Totals
	Text	Tab	Full	Part	Full	Part	
Operating instructions							
Introduction	0.5						0.5
Controls and indicators	0.5	0.5			1.0		2.0
Turn-on procedure	0.5						0.5
Turn-off procedure	0.5						0.5
Normal operating procedure	1.5						1.5
Subtotal	3.5	0.5		—	1.0	—	5.0
Theory of Operation							
Introduction	0.5						0.5
Overall functional description	1.5		1.0				2.5
Detailed functional description	3.0	—		3.0			6.0
Subtotal	5.0		1.0	3.0	—	—	9.0

TABLE 5-3 A Cost Estimating Matrix used to Determine Page Counts (Cont.)

Description	PAGE UNITS		LINE ART		TONE ART		Totals
	Text	Tab	Full	Part	Full	Part	
Maintenance procedures							
Introduction	0.5						0.5
Tools and test equipment	0.5	1.0					1.5
Operator-level maintenance	1.0	0.5					1.5
Preventive maintenance	0.5						0.5
Cleaning and inspection	0.5	0.5	1.0				2.0
Minimum performance standards	0.5	2.5	2.0				5.0
Corrective maintenance	0.5						0.5
Fault isolation	0.5	3.0	2.0				5.5
Disassembly procedures	2.5		2.0				4.5
Reassembly procedures	0.5						0.5
Subtotal	7.5	7.5	7.0	—	—		22.0
Parts list							
Introduction	0.5						0.5
Parts information	0.5	8.0		—	7.0	3.0	18.5
Subtotal	1.0	8.0	—	—	7.0	3.0	19.0
Diagrams							
Introduction	0.5						0.5
Types of diagrams	0.5	0.5					1.0
Terms and symbols	1.0			1.0			2.0
Diagrams			5.0	3.0			8.0
Subtotal	2.0	0.5	5.0	4.0	—	—	11.5
Total	28.0	23.5	17.0	7.0	8.0	4.0	87.5

Description	PAGE UNITS		LINE ART		TONE ART		Totals
	Text	Tab	Full	Part	Full	Part	
User's booklet							
Front matter	1.0	2.0	1.0				4.0
Introduction	1.0						1.0
Operating procedures	2.0				2.0		4.0
In case of trouble	1.0	0.5					1.5
Total	5.0	2.5	1.0	——	2.0	——	10.5
Grand total	33.0	26.0	18.0	7.0	10.0	4.0	98.0

Notes:
Deduct partial illustrations from raw total to determine total pages:
Full pages = raw total - 0.5(partial line + partial tone)

Service manual: 87.5 - 0.5(7 + 4) = 82
User's manual: 10.5 - 0.5(0 + 0) = 10.5 (Round to 11)
Total pages this project: 94

covered by a picture and table, each cable has a list and illustration section in the parts list chapter and a wiring diagram in the diagrams chapter, and so on.

PREPARING THE FINAL COST ESTIMATE

We now have enough information to begin our cost estimate. The estimated page and illustration counts can be combined with our standard labor multipliers to determine the number of hours by labor category. Next, we will multiply the labor hours by the approved pay rates to get direct labor dollars. We will add material and travel costs and then mark up the labor and material with the appropriate overhead rates. To this we will add the general and administrative rate and profit to get our selling price.

Let us perform our estimate using the data in Tables 5-1 through 5-3; the specification, maintenance, and product description; and the following assumptions:

1. There will be one in-process review.
2. There will be one prepublication review.
3. There will be one $560 trip associated with the service manual.
4. The deliverable item is camera-ready reproducible copy (no printing charges required).
5. The complexity of the user's booklet is considered simple.
6. The complexity of the service manual is average.
7. The quality of source material is satisfactory.

The Process

Tables 5-4 and 5-5 show how the multipliers are used in conjunction with the page count to determine hours and dollars. The actual process is developed as follows:

TABLE 5-4 Cost-Estimating Matrix

Description	PAGE UNITS						Sub-total Hours	In-Proc Review	Pre-Prod. Review	Total Hours	Labor Rate	Direct Dollars
	Text		Line Art		Tone Art							
	Text	Tab	Full	Part	Full	Part						
Service manual pages:	28.0	23.5	17.0	7.0	8.0	4.0						
Write	112.0	117.5	59.5	28.0	16.0	8.0	341.0	361.0	398.0	398.0	14.23	5933.91
Project admin.							17.0	18.0	19.9	19.9	14.23	270.37
Edit	8.4	9.4	3.2	0.7	0.8	0.4	22.9		25.9	25.9	13.1	341.36
Prod. edit	5.6	4.7	3.4	0.7	1.6	0.8	16.8		18.5	18.5	12.76	236.06
Draft type	8.4	14.1	1.7	3.5	0.4	0.2	28.3		31.1	31.1	5.90	183.49
Typeset	14.0	18.8	5.1	1.4	0.4	0.2	39.9		43.9	43.9	8.54	374.91
Proofread	8.4	9.4	3.2	0.7	0.4	0.2	22.3		24.5	24.5	6.95	170.28
Illustrate			102.0	21.0	24.0	6.0	153.0		168.0	168.0	9.20	1546.60
Paste up	14.0	14.1	5.1	1.05	1.6	0.4	36.2		40.0	40.0	8.76	350.40
Totals										769.9		9964.45

TABLE 5-4 Cost-Estimating Matrix (Cont.)

Description	PAGE UNITS						Sub-total Hours	In-Proc Review	Pre-Prod. Review	Total Hours	Labor Rate	Direct Dollars
	Text		Line Art		Tone Art							
	Text	Tab	Full	Part	Full	Part						
User's manual												
pages	5.0	2.5	1.0		2.0							
Write	20.0	25.0	4.0		4.0		53.0					
Complexity factor							*31.8	33.7	37.0	37.0	14.23	526.51
Project admin.							1.6	1.7	1.9	1.9	14.23	27.04
Edit	1.5	1.0	0.2		0.2		2.9		3.2	3.2	13.18	42.18
Prod. edit	1.0	0.5	0.2		0.4		2.1		2.3	2.3	12.76	29.35
Draft type	1.5	1.5	0.1		0.1		3.2		3.5	3.5	5.90	20.77
Typeset	2.5	2.0	0.3		0.1		4.9		5.4	5.4	8.54	46.12
Proofread	1.5	1.0	0.2		0.1		2.8		3.1	3.1	6.95	21.55
Illustrate			6.0		6.0		12.0		13.2	13.2	9.20	121.44
Paste up	2.5	1.5	0.3		0.4		4.7		5.2	5.2	8.76	45.55
Totals										74.8		880.51

* Complexity factor: 53 total writer hours x 0.6

TABLE 5-5 Adding Overhead and Markup to Direct Costs

PROJECT	SERVICE MANUAL	USER'S MANUAL
Direct labor	$ 9,964.45	$ 880.51
Overhead @ 80%	7,971.64	704.41
Subtotal	$17,936.09	$1,584.92
Material and travel	560.00	0.00
Overhead @ 10%	56.00	0.00
Subtotal	$ 616.00	$ 0.00
Total direct costs	$18,552.09	$1,584.92
General and administrative		
Costs @ 20%	3,710.42	316.98
Subtotal	22,262.51	1,901.90
Profit or fee @ 15%	3,339.38	285.29
Total selling price	$25,601.89	$2,187.19
	==========	=========

1. The pages are multiplied by the hours per page for each labor category.
2. Review, complexity, and administrative cost multipliers are used to adjust the hours.
3. The labor hours are multiplied by the established labor rates.
4. The labor dollars are summed to determine total direct labor dollars.
5. Labor overhead is applied to the direct labor dollars and subtotaled.
6. Material and travel dollars are computed.
7. Material and travel overhead is applied to the material and travel and subtotaled.
8. Direct labor and overhead is added to material and travel and overhead.
9. The total of step 8 is multiplied by the general and administrative rate and subtotaled.
10. The subtotal from step 9 is multiplied by the profit rate, and the final selling price is established.

11. Standard comparisons can be established, such as dollars per page or hours per page. These help to determine how the estimate compares with other similar projects where cost data is available.

12. Once the final estimate is complete, the profit margin for the job can be determined using the standard formula.

If we wish to determine how our estimate compares with those of other projects in gross terms, we can calculate the dollars per page and the total hours per page. Hours per page are compared by dividing the total hours by the number of pages in each book. The dollars per page are calculated by dividing the total dollars at either price or cost level by the number of pages. Our numbers are as follows:

	DIRECT LABOR		MLO*	@ PRICE
	Hours/Page	Dollars/Page	Dollars/Page	Dollars/Page
Service manual	769.9/82	$9,964.45/82	$18,552.09/82	$25,601.89/82
	9.39	$121.52	$226.24	$312.22
User's manual	74.8/11	$880.51/11	$1,584.92/11	$2,187.19/11
	6.8	$80.05	$144.08	$198.84

* MLO is an abbreviation of material, labor, and overhead.

CALCULATING THE GROSS PROFIT MARGIN

The other calculation that is usually made is the gross profit margin (GPM). The formula used to calculate the GPM is

$$\frac{price - cost \times 100}{price} = \% \text{ gross profit margin}$$

The profit margin can be estimated at the organizational level, which often includes direct labor, material, and overhead as cost, and excludes the general and administrative burden. Regardless of the method used, it is important to be consistent to ensure "apples-to-apples" comparisons. The direct labor, material, and overhead GPM associated with the manuals are described as follows:

$$\text{service manual \% GPM} = \frac{\$25,601.89 - \$18,552.09}{\$25,601.89} = 27.54\%$$

$$\text{user's manual \% GPM} = \frac{\$2,187.19 - \$1,584.92}{\$2,187.19} = 27.54\%$$

These are the same because the added general and administrative and profit values are identical for both manuals. The 27.5 percent level is sometimes expressed as "par value" GPM, since it is a goal for the operating department. Falling below the par level means that the project is experiencing an overrun. Beating par means the job was accomplished in less time or with less funding than was originally estimated.

Padding a Cost Estimate

It may be tempting for cost estimators who know that they are estimating a project that is "in the bag" to "pad" their estimates. In this way, they increase the probability of making or exceeding par GPM. This should never be done!

The cost estimator's job is to estimate the project as accurately as possible. It is upper management's prerogative to make price adjustments, but these individuals must have the facts to act intelligently. Finally, the price must often be defended in contract negotiations. A negotiator will lose credibility if he or she must defend a set of inflated numbers.

REVIEW QUESTIONS

1. What are *cost multipliers*?

2. What factors influence cost multipliers?

3. Draw a cost multiplier table of your own for the writing, editing, and typing functions, where text pages require

   3 hour to write
   0.5 hour to edit
   0.4 hour to type

   and illustrations pages require

   6 hours to write
   1 hour to edit
   0.2 hour to type

4. Determine the cost of a 10-page, 2-illustration booklet from your cost multiplier table, where writing is $25.00 per hour, editing is $20.00 per hour, and typing is $12.00 per hour.

5. Why should cost estimating rate schedules be handled as company classified information?

6. List six *other costs.*

7. What is *labor overhead*?

8. What is *profit*?

9. Mark up $1,000 of direct labor using 80 percent overhead, 20 percent general and administrative expenses, and 15 percent profit.

10. Define the phrase *depth of coverage.*

11. Define the phrase *subject matter complexity.*

12. What is meant by *maintenance philosophy*?

13. Draw an *estimating matrix* of your own for a simple user's booklet based on the contents of Table 5-3. Develop your own page count.

14. Estimate the price of your booklet using the multipliers in Tables 5-4 and 5-5.

15. Calculate the *gross profit margin* of your user's booklet.

6

Publications Contract Negotiations

INTRODUCTION

In Chapter 5 we described the cost-estimating process. Once a cost estimate has been developed and submitted, the next step in the process is contract negotiations. Contract negotiations involve the buyer and seller bargaining in good faith. Each party's objective is to reach what they believe is a reasonable price for the product under consideration. The seller, who has estimated the cost required to deliver the product, must negotiate a price at which his or her company can make a profit. The buyer tries to negotiate a price that he or she believes to be fair. This chapter describes the contract negotiation process.

TYPES OF CONTRACTS

There are several types of contracts used in the procurement of technical literature. These include

1. Firm fixed-price contracts
2. Time and material contracts
3. Cost plus fixed fee
4. Cost plus incentive fee

Each of these is briefly described in the following paragraphs.

Firm Fixed-Price Contracts

A firm fixed-price contract is one in which both parties agree upon a fixed price for the work to be performed. Regardless of the cost of the project, the buyer and seller are guaranteed a fixed price. The risk is minimal for the buyer; it is maximum for the seller. The seller's risk involves the accuracy of the project cost estimate and potential overruns. Another area of risk resides in the language of the contract terms and conditions. If the buyer is a stickler for details and creates an inordinate amount of rework in the review process, he or she can "break the bank." On the other hand, if the seller has included contingencies for the risks involved, an excellent level of profit may be achieved.

Time and Material Contracts

A time and material contract is fundamentally a service-type contract, where the buyer purchases labor and material at an agreed-upon rate. Here, the risk is minimal for the seller, who will be reimbursed for every hour of labor and every dollar of material expenditure. The labor rates normally include profit, and material charges most often include handling markup. The advantage of a time and material contract for a buyer is that the contract can be terminated within a specified period of time called out in the contract. For example, many contracts state that either party can cancel the contract upon 10 to 30 days' written notice.

Cost Plus Fixed-Fee Contract

A cost plus fixed-fee contract is normally worded to reimburse the seller for all costs expended in the performance of a contract. A fixed fee, or profit, is normally established in the language of the contract. The fee can be a specified amount or a percentage of the cost depending on the terms and conditions.

A cost plus fixed-fee (CPFF) contract can have an established cost ceiling. Once the ceiling is reached, the cost rate can change, or the seller and the buyer may begin a cost-sharing formula.

For example, a fixed fee of $15,000 may be the reward for delivering a publications project at a cost of $100,000. If the cost exceeds $100,000, the seller will forfeit $1.00 for every $2.00 overrun. If the project reaches $130,000, the seller may be required to bear the total burden of the overrun.

The variations in the terms of the contract shift the risk from buyer to seller, and therefore the fees and percentages are normally negotiated based on the perceived risk.

Cost Plus Incentive Fee

A cost plus incentive fee (CPIF) contract normally rewards the seller for minimizing costs. The incentive fee can also be based on delivery schedule or a combination of cost minimization and schedule.

For example, if the seller maintains contract cost below $100,000, he or she will receive a 15 percent fee. If the contract is between $100,000 and $150,000, the fee will be 8 percent. Hence the higher the cost, the lower the profit. The incentive is for the seller to minimize the cost and thereby receive a larger fee. Again, the risk depends on the specific terms and the base of experience upon which the cost estimate has been made.

THE PROPOSAL AND COST QUOTATION PROCESS

Proposals are submitted in many ways and include many kinds of information. Proposals can include a technical solution to a buyer's problem, a cost quotation, and an overview of the seller's organization, major customers, key personnel, financial status, and capabilities.

Proposals can be solicited by potential buyers, or they can be submitted by a seller on an unsolicited basis. Solicited proposals normally include guidelines including a preliminary contract, statement of work, and specifications.

The company submitting a proposal normally prepares a written response to the request for proposal in the format requested. Failure to address all items requested often results in a potential seller being designated nonresponsive, which may disqualify him or her as a bidder. In the case of governmental agencies, proposals are normally required by the close of business at a specified agency address on a specified date. Failure to comply with all facets of the request for proposal and quotation will normally result in disqualification of the bidder.

Once all proposals are received by the buyer, they are compared. The bidder with the most attractive solution and price is normally selected. Once selected, the negotiation process begins.

THE NEGOTIATION PROCESS

Many experienced contract negotiators consider face-to-face price and term negotiations the cream of the negotiation process. However, it is the shortest lived. The entire process requires an extensive amount of preparation and hard work.

The phases of the negotiation process generally include

1. Preparation
2. Fact-finding
3. Contract negotiations
4. Contract approval

These phases are sometimes conducted in one brief meeting if the project is relatively small. However, on a large contract, the process may last for weeks and even months.

Preparation

The preparation phase of contract negotiations includes the collection of all pertinent contract documents, statements of work, cost estimates, review of the labor and material to be delivered to ensure a working knowledge, research into similar efforts to determine risks, and the establishment of a strategy that will defend the price being offered. This process is conducted by both the buyer and seller.

A price goal is normally established by both parties. The seller sets a minimum and ideal price; the buyer sets a desired and not-to-exceed price. Once the research is complete and each party has his or her review notes and preliminary numbers in mind, they begin the fact-finding process.

Fact-Finding

The fact-finding phase involves both parties in a meeting with their technical and contract experts to ensure that both parties agree upon the meaning and intent of the contract language. They investigate the size of the task to ensure that all details are thoroughly understood. Changes in terms, conditions, or specifications that may be objectionable to either party are discussed. Where possible, new language is hammered out to the satisfaction of both parties. Let us look at some of the details that are often discussed during the fact-finding process.

Justifying the Cost. It is up to the seller to establish a valid basis for the initial publications price quotation in page count and corresponding labor and material. This is where a good publications cost estimator shines. By being able to go through an outline of the proposed book and discuss specific content and corresponding text, tables, and illustrations, the buyer is assured that the seller understands the task at hand, has scoped it accurately, and is prepared to commit the necessary resources to get the job done.

Cost Multipliers and the Benefit of Productivity. Once the page count is established, the parties review the labor multipliers. When both are experienced, they know what costs should be. Hours per page and dollars per page are common standards used in fact-finding. If the seller happens to employ automated processes, such as word processors and high-speed, programmable photocomposers, they will be rewarded for their productivity. They can sell their product at accepted market value while keeping their cost well below the market rate. Obviously, productivity pays in profit.

Deliverable Items. The parties also examine deliverable items. The deliverable item can take several forms. Common publications submittal forms are

1. Manuscript form (draft typed) with hand-drawn sketches and glossy prints of line drawings and photographic artwork
2. Camera-ready, reproducible copy (ready for printing) of all text and illustrations
3. Photolithographic negatives of all text and illustration pages suitable for printing plate generation
4. Items 2 and 3
5. Printed copies in the quantity specified by the contract
6. A printed copy packed with each item of equipment
7. Items 2, 3, and 5

The form chosen depends on how the customer plans on reproducing and distributing the publication. If the buyer has an in-house typesetting and art department, item 1 may be the choice. If the customer has a printing operation, such as the Government Printing Office, he or she may wish to purchase either items 2 or 3. Some buyers purchase publications from several different subcontractors under a single prime contract arrangement.

For example, a major aircraft manufacturer may purchase equipment and supporting publications from numerous suppliers of communications, radar, navigation, and airframe component manufacturers. To keep the publications common in appearance, they may decide to purchase manuscript and sketches and produce the publications themselves. In addition, their own labor and material content will be higher. By maximizing their own *value added*, they are able to increase profits. On the other hand, if they are resource bound, they may have their subcontractors supply printed books.

Change-in-Scope. A change-in-scope occurs when the buyer or seller requires the seller to perform some task that is outside of the original contract agreement or when the seller fails to perform a contractual obligation. When this happens, the parties may call for a change-in-scope adjustment, which either adds to or reduces the established price.

For example, the buyer may require the seller to submit more review copies than initially specified. If this happens, the supplier may reopen the price of review copies, asking for more money. Usually, some latitude is allowed by both parties. However, some people habitually take advantage of a seller's (or buyer's) goodwill. To keep from being "nickle and dimed to death," one of the parties may put his or her foot down and ask for a change-in-scope fee.

Schedules. The schedules are clearly defined by milestone charts and other documents that are part of the contract or statement of work. Schedules can have significant impact on costs. If the contract is "short fused," requiring that the publication be expedited, the efficiency of the writing and production effort may be affected. For example, if a 24-person month writing effort is packed into an 8-month period, it will require between three and four writers. None will be "up the learning curve." This means that they will not be efficient. The inefficiency will penalize the seller's cost, and therefore the 24-person month effort may actually cost 32 person-months. Other expedite charges may be felt in the production areas, especially when large blocks of overtime are required to complete the project on schedule.

Summary. Once the page count, labor hours, and rates are acceptable to both parties and deliverable items, policies on change-in-scope, and schedules have been discussed and are understood by both parties, they are ready to proceed to the next stage, contract negotiations. Negotiations sometimes happen immediately. Other times the parties involved establish a future date for the negotiation process and return to their home offices to prepare.

Contract Negotiations

Once the fact-finding process is over, the parties are ready to get down to hard negotiating. There are times when the fact-finding process answers all questions and the buyer settles for the initial asking price. However, when big dollars and contract terms are at stake, the negotiation process normally includes some heavy haggling between the parties.

The Seller's Position. Before entering into hard negotiations, it is necessary to have a thorough understanding of all costs expected in the performance of the contracted work in addition to any risks associated with the project. Something that is sometimes overlooked is the cost to the business in committing its valuable resources for the contract period. If other, more profitable, work is available during the same time frame, the asking price should be enough to make allocation of your resources worthwhile.

Every selling negotiator approaches the bargaining table with a "bottom price" level in mind and concessions that he or she is prepared to make. The seller also has a price goal — the price at which his or her company can minimize its risk and maximize its profit.

The selling negotiator has a list of jeopardy items considered "risky." These are tools to be used in justifying a higher price, improved conditions, early progress payments, or an above-average profit percentage. Experienced negotiators hold them in reserve, throwing them on the table one at a time with precision timing. They are used to defend positions and to attack weaknesses.

The Buyer's Position.   As does the selling negotiator, the buying   negotiator   has   specific   goals   too.   These   include purchasing   goods   at   a   fair   price,   obtaining   terms   that   are consistent   with   the   buyer's   company's   business   objectives, such as schedule and quality assurance levels, and ensuring that the buyer is protected in the event that the seller is unable to comply with the terms of the contract. The buyer also must ensure that product acceptance is based on his or her terms, not the seller's.

The buyer also comes to the table armed. Looking back on the fact-finding process, the buyer has notes that show where the seller has overestimated certain areas of the project. These are used to break down any positions of risk presented by the seller. In addition, the buyer uses precedence, such as dollars   per   page,   hours   per   illustration,   and   any   other guidelines that can support a case for lowering the price.

The Bargaining Process.   Many   bargaining   sessions   are more a matter of formality than a negotiation. The parties have hammered out the basic details during the bidding and fact-finding process, and they are ready to wrap up the loose ends and   get   started.   However,   some   are   dramatic   and   even strenuous.

Armed with bales of documentation and calculators, the buyer and the seller begin the process. A high-stake negotiation often becomes a contest of wills and wits. Both buyer and seller know the rules. No treachery; no lies; perhaps a little acting   with   the   look   of   shock,   dismay,   or   wrinkled-brow concern used to make a point or emphasize a position. The bout can range from charm, jokes, and sincerity, to anger. Each party uses everything at hand to be as convincing and persuasive as possible. They use their personalities, emotions, and gestures to make their points. And, as in poker, neither side wants the other to know what kind of hand they are holding. Never show the next card until it is time to lay it on the table.

Both may have "star witnesses" waiting in the wings. When negotiating teams represent each side, they may break for frequent conferences to decide on how to respond to new offers or requests or to discuss strategies and counterstrategies. The negotiation may go on for days, even weeks. Phone calls are made to the home office. People are flown in to discuss some technical detail upon which a major issue hinges.

Once all the details are agreed upon, the terms settled, and schedules established, the final item discussed is normally the profit level. "Your fee of 15 percent is out of the question," the buyer may say. "We never pay more than 8 percent on a contract like this."

The seller responds, "Even though we both agree that the cost level is $123,000, there's just too much risk. The only way we're going to cover ourselves is with a 15 percent fee. Otherwise, we'll lose money on this job."

"Look," says the buyer, "we agreed that the cost was real — it comprehends your risk. There's no way we can accept risk in your fee. Your fee is pure markup based on everyone's understanding of cost. We can only pay 8 percent profit."

The seller shakes his head soberly and sighs. "My company has never sold a project for under 10 percent, and we normally get 20. As it stands, 15 percent is a very reasonable offer. Anyway, there's no way my management would approve anything close to 8 percent."

The buyers huddle. "Okay," the buyer's spokesperson says, "Look, it doesn't appear that we're going to get anywhere.

We're here trying to bargain in good faith and you won't bargain. So that we can wrap this thing up and get out of here, we'll offer 9 percent."

The seller leans back, slaps his forehead, closes his eyes, and shakes his head in disbelief. He then turns in his chair and discusses the offer with the members of his team. "Thirteen percent," he announces, studying the buyer's expressionless face for a sign. "Look," the seller continues, "I'm bargaining in good faith. I've gone as far as I can go by conceding two percentage points of profit. I don't know what else I can do. I've gone further than I planned we'd have to go. We actually planned on 15 percent—14 as a rock bottom. Now here I am at 13; that's it."

The process continues like this. In this illustration, the contract is probably settled at 11 ½ or 12 percent. Once agreed, everyone compliments each other, shakes hands, and the contracts are drafted as negotiated.

Contract Approval

The contract approval process is necessary to make all agreements legal and binding. Once the contracts are drafted as agreed upon by the negotiating teams, each party obtains the signature of an authorized company officer. There are instances when a designated company officer decides that the agreement is not in the best interest of his company. This is rare, but it does happen.

To prevent this from happening, the involved contract negotiators should always ensure that all major contract conditions are understood by authorizing officers before they are settled at the bargaining table. It is common for negotiating teams to break for a phone call to ensure that all terms and conditions are agreeable to everyone back at the home office.

When a failure to obtain approval does occur, it sometimes means that negotiations must be reopened. There are times when only company officers, themselves, can settle the final conditions. The decisions may be beyond the authorization of the negotiating parties. Again, this is rare; however, it does happen.

REVIEW QUESTIONS

1. Describe a *firm fixed-price contract.*
2. What is a *time and material contract?*
3. What is a *cost plus fixed-fee contract?*
4. Describe a *cost plus incentive fee contract.*
5. What is the difference between a *solicited* and an *unsolicited* proposal?
6. List the four phases of the contract negotiation process.
7. What is a *price goal* and who establishes it?
8. What is the purpose of fact-finding?
9. What is a *change-in-scope?*
10. Describe the leverage of risk.

7

Cost
Control
and Reporting

INTRODUCTION

The cost-estimating and contract negotiation processes were described in Chapters 5 and 6. Once the estimate is complete and all contractual matters are settled, it is time to begin the project. However, of equal importance, it is time to start controlling project expenditures. This is done by knowing beforehand what the labor, material, and overhead rates are; establishing review and approval procedures for project expenditures before they happen, and having a cost collection system that tells you how much money you are spending, on what it is being spent, and when. This chapter describes

1. Establishing a project budget and schedule
2. Cost-reporting systems
3. Cost-control responsibilities
4. The importance of project financial reviews
5. The impact of available information on cost standards
6. Customer cost control

ESTABLISHING A PROJECT BUDGET AND SCHEDULE

Every project should have a clearly understood budget and schedule before the work is begun. The budget and schedule provide goals for everyone to work toward. If the project is staffed by several people, it is a good idea to call a project meeting, go over the work to be performed, discuss the schedule, and if considered appropriate, show the cost goals. The cost goals do not have to be discussed in dollars and cents. They can be shown in hours, weeks, or person months. To make the discussion meaningful, the required number of written, edited, or typeset pages per day can be discussed. This way, the involved people can know what is expected, and know when they are ahead or behind schedule. The probability for meeting goals is much greater when each person has an individual challenge.

The original cost estimate and results of the contract negotiation process can be used as background for establishing the project budget. The budget should generally be agressive to meet or exceed cost and profit goals. It should be broken out in categories, such as labor hours by writer, editor, illustrator, typist, and so on. Material charges should be anticipated. Time frames should be established also. From this, a "running rate" can be computed. Knowing that you have $30,000 dollars to spend in six months says that you can spend $5,000 per month. If you exceed the running rate in the first few months, it is clear that you must spend less in later months. The running rate gives you a good rule of thumb to follow.

Often, the budget is written down on a "spreadsheet" similar to that shown in Figure 7-1. In addition, an accompanying chart like the one shown in Figure 7-1 can be developed to show forecasted and actual expenditures. This format is designed to highlight graphically variances to the budget.

COST-REPORTING SYSTEMS

Cost-reporting systems are used to collect cost information against specific projects, organize the information in an easy-to-read format, and distribute the information to the responsible people. Each of these facets is examined in the following paragraphs.

Cost Collection

Before costs can be effectively controlled, they must be collected. There are numerous ways in which to collect

Project Name: __7660 Actuator Manual__
Budgeted by: __Sam Smith__ Date: __10/21/1982__
Approved by: __Bill Madison__ Date: __10/24/1982__

Description	JAN	FEB	MAR	APR	MAY	JUN	JUL	AUG	TOTAL MN MO	TOTAL $K
Write	0.5	1.0	1.0	1.0	1.0	0.5	0.5	0.2	5.7	$14.25
Edit	0.1	0.1	0.1	0.2	0.2	0.2	1.0	0.5	2.4	5.16
Illustrate	0.0	0.5	1.0	1.0	0.5	0.2	0.2	0.1	3.5	6.30
Composition	0.0	0.0	0.0	0.0	0.5	1.5	1.0	0.2	3.2	3.84
Photography		0.5							0.5	0.90
Print							1.2	3.3	4.5	7.65
Other										
Subtotal	0.6	2.1	2.1	2.2	2.2	2.4	3.9	4.3	19.8	$38.10

	JAN	FEB	MAR	APR	MAY	JUN	JUL	AUG		
Overhead										30.48
Total direct labor	2.1	7.3	7.3	7.6	7.6	8.3	13.5	14.9		68.58
Material										0.00
Material overhead										0.00
Travel			1.2K			1.2K				2.40
Total	2.1	7.3	8.5	7.6	7.6	9.5	13.5	14.9		$70.98

Dollars ($K)	JAN	FEB	MAR	APR	MAY	JUN	JUL	AUG	SEP	OCT
$100										
90										
80										
70										
60										
50										
40										
30										
20										
10										
0										

Plan ( )										
Monthly	2.1	7.3	8.5	7.6	7.6	9.5	13.5	14.9		
Cumulative	2.1	9.4	17.9	25.5	33.1	42.6	56.1	71.0		
Actual ( )										
Monthly	1.5	6.0	7.0	9.2	10.3	11.2	14.6	15.0		
Cumulative year to date	1.5	7.5	14.5	23.7	34.0	45.2	59.8	74.8		
Variance										
Monthly	0.6	1.3	1.5	-1.6	-2.7	-1.7	-1.1	-0.1		
Cumulative 2 years to date	0.6	1.9	3.4	1.8	-0.9	-2.6	-3.7	-3.8		

FIGURE 7-1 Budget Spreadsheet and Variance Analysis

charges against a project. The systems used range from manual entry systems, where material receipts and timesheets are manually collected and tabulated, to sophisticated data processing systems, where the same information is collected and tabulated with the help of a computer system. Regardless of the level of sophistication, all time and material must be compiled and computed.

The people working on a project normally charge their time in established standard cost units, such as dollars per hour, week, or month. All material purchased, if considered a direct charge against the project, must be tabulated. However, if the material is purchased as a general department supply used by several projects, then it may be partially allocated to the project as overhead expense. Whether a charge is direct or overhead depends on accounting guidelines established by the company's Control Department. The method is unimportant. What is important is that all legitimate charges are known, written down, and made available in a timely manner.

Timeliness

Timeliness is an important part of the cost collection system. Excessive system delays can allow a budget to get out of control before anyone is aware that a problem exists. By the time you find out, it may be too late.

This is where computerized cost-collection and reporting systems are valuable. Once the input data are available, the system can collect, tabulate, and print a project cost summary as well as a detail report in a matter of minutes.

Reporting

The reports used vary widely from company to company; however, they should be in a meaningful, easy-to-read form. The information should include both current period and year-to-date time periods. It is important to know exactly what the "cut-off" date for the charges is, such as the last day of the prior month, or some other date specified on the report.

Another important feature of a cost report is having a breakdown of labor charges by effort type, such as direct dollars for writing, editing, typesetting, illustrating, and so on. This is normally accomplished by establishing an "effort code system," which allows those charging time to the project to write down their effort code as well as the number of hours they charged to the job.

Similarly, material expenditures should be reported with sufficient descriptive information to determine specific material costs. Both money spent with vendors as well as open commitments with estimated amounts to be spent should be available. Without this kind of breakdown, it is difficult to know where the money is going or how much additional financial commitment exists, without an extensive, time-consuming audit.

COST-CONTROL RESPONSIBILITIES

In most companies, the project manager is normally responsible for seeing that the costs are controlled. The budget is essentially a cost goal that the project manager tries to achieve. The project manager's performance depends to a great extent on his or her ability to deliver the product on schedule and within budget.

It is often a good idea to delegate subordinate budget responsibility on large programs so that others working on the project will assist the project manager in meeting cost goals. For example, if a project has two or more major subdivisions, such as hardware manuals, software manuals, and merchandising literature, you may assign budget responsibility to a "lead" person in each area. Each month, you can have a project review and have each person report on his or her particular part of the budget. In this manner, you not only have help in budget control, but you are developing your people by teaching them financial control. This prepares them for increased responsibility.

A cost file should be maintained with all financial information. Each month, the responsible project manager should record the cost-to-date and forecast project cost-to-complete and cost-at-completion information. A form similar to the one shown in Figure 7-2 might be used to record this kind of information. It not only shows the original forecast, cost-to-date, cost-to-complete, and cost-at-completion data, it also shows the quality of the forecasting from month to month. By knowing that the forecast and actuals will be compared each month, those making the forecasts tend to be more conscientious with their numbers.

Forecast Date	JAN	FEB	MAR	APR	MAY	JUN	JUL	CTD	CTC	CAC
Forecast	2.1	7.3	7.3	7.6	7.6	8.3	13.5	0	53.7	53.7
January	1.8	7.6	7.3	7.6	7.6	8.3	13.5	1.8	51.9	53.7
February	1.8	7.4	7.5	7.6	7.6	8.3	13.5	9.2	44.5	53.7
March	1.8	7.4	7.1	7.5	7.5	8.3	13.5	16.3	36.8	53.1
April	1.8	7.4	7.1	7.7	7.5	8.3	13.5	24.0	29.3	53.3
May	1.8	7.4	7.1	7.7	7.7	8.3	13.5	31.7	21.8	53.5
June	1.8	7.4	7.1	7.7	7.7	9.0	12.9	40.7	12.9	53.6
July (final)	1.8	7.4	7.1	7.7	7.7	9.0	13.6	54.3	0	54.3

Notes:

CTD = cost to date.
CTC = cost to complete.
CAC = cost at completion.

FIGURE 7-2 Monthly Project Cost-Forecasting Form

THE IMPORTANCE OF PROJECT FINANCIAL REVIEWS

The popular adage, "You can expect what you inspect," indicates one of the values of having regularly scheduled project financial reviews. When project managers know that someone will be looking at the financial status of their project, they tend to pay careful attention to their budget. It is human nature to want to demonstrate one's capability as a manager, and project managers get that chance in a financial review, if his or her budget is on target. If it is not, then the project manager is expected to know why. Financial reviews, then, can be a form of control as well as a form of recognition.

Another beneficial function of financial reviews is that they serve as a valuable communications medium. When problems exist, upper-level managers can be told about them. If the problem is organizational or resource related, resolution may require the help of a senior manager. By the same token, upper-level managers identify problems and, in doing so, enlist the help of their people toward the solutions.

Financial reviews also serve as a platform for the discussion of good business practices and policy-related matters. Upper-level managers may detect situations that are contrary to accepted business practices or company policy. When they do, they can instruct those in attendance of the proper methods and procedures. Project financial reviews can provide an element of instructional value. In summary, project financial reviews

1. Encourage project managers to meet their budgetary commitments
2. Serve as a form of recognition
3. Provide a two-way communications medium
4. Enlist the help of upper-level managers in problem solving
5. Enlist the help of lower-level managers in problem solving
6. Serve as an instructional medium

THE IMPACT OF AVAILABLE INFORMATION ON COST STANDARDS

The process of using cost standards as a basis for budgets, monitoring the financial performance of the project by comparing forecasted cost data to actual cost data using forms similar to the one shown in Figure 7-2, and discussing the financial performance in financial review meetings helps to refine existing cost standards.

Establishing New Standards

When an operation is new, or completely revamped, it is necessary to perform an industrial engineering analysis to estimate expected performance levels. Once the theoretical throughput level is determined in units per hour or some other similar standard, effective throughput must be estimated. For example, if a typesetter has a speed of 985 lines of type per minute, the theoretical throughput of the typesetter running at full capacity would be 60 × 985, or 59,100 lines per hour. Of course, the analysis then must comprehend file loading time, font change time, idle time, paper change time, downtime for repair or preventive maintenance, operator break and meal time, and all the other delays associated with machine operation. The 985- line-per-minute typesetter may have an effective throughput rate of 50 lines per minute when everything is taken into consideration.

Therefore, it is vital to put a dimension of reality in the equation when establishing new productivity standards. Once the standards are established, the feedback of actual operation should be used to update the standards. These standards should be kept realistic. If anything, they should be slightly on the aggressive side. Those performing the work should know what the standards are so they can be used as goals.

The standards should serve as a basis for cost estimating. If the standards are overly aggressive, cost estimates will be low, causing overruns. If they are too lenient, cost estimates will be high, and that may cause a contract negotiator to lose credibility. As a result, productivity and cost standards must be as accurate as possible.

Reviewing and Modifying Existing Standards

The refinement of cost standards should be a continuous process. Techniques change, experience changes, and processes and equipment are upgraded. All these change the throughput capability of any production-type operation. Using new techniques or improved materials, for example, may reduce the time required to perform an operation. Experience itself, referred to as the "learning curve," lets people do things more efficiently as they improve their job skills. What at one time was awkward becomes easy and natural with practice. Not only do they become more proficient with experience, they reduce rework levels and scrap, reducing the cost of both labor and material. Finally, modern automated equipment often replaces old manual equipment. This too increases throughput and cuts unit cost. The feedback provided by actual cost information helps "fine-tune" cost multipliers, keeping them abreast of current technologies.

CUSTOMER COST CONTROL

Perhaps one of the most difficult tasks of a project manager is to keep his or her customer in control. Customers often have a tendency to expect little "extras." These can include such things as extra review copies, extra trips (either by you to the customer's facility or by the customer to your facility), advance photographs or drawings of the product, and so on. These may all sound like inconsequential things, but some customers take advantage of a vendor's good-will and wind up "nickel and diming" the vendor to death. The result: all these expenses come right out of profit; therefore, lower profits accrue to your company.

If you let the customer begin this course of "freebies," you will find it quite difficult to shut him or her off. On the other hand, if you let the customer know that the request is a "change-in-scope" to the terms and conditions of the contract and discuss a fee for the extra services, the customer will think twice before asking for future favors.

You should not feel awkward when you remind the customer that favors are outside your contractual agreement. You are in a business situation. Agreeing to give extras is the same as giving away company assets. You might remind the customer that you do not have authority to hand over extras, and that you must get approval from upper management. This in itself may discourage additional requests.

Another facet of customer control is to ensure compliance with scheduled milestones. If the customer causes delays, you may have to extend the project schedule, resulting in increased costs as a result of additional time consumed in waiting. If you stop work, you will find inefficiencies in restarting the job. Materials may become obsolete or lost. Your people will have to "ramp up" again when it is time to restart the effort. One of the easiest ways to lose money, and perhaps one of the most common, is to extend a schedule.

Schedule delays should be treated as a change in scope. Estimate the loss in efficiency. The potential of losing key people to another project can kill your chances for a profitable project. In addition, you may wind up jeopardizing other projects when they are yanked back to the original one. All these costs must be considered, and the customer should be apprised of them before you agree to delay project milestones.

SUMMARY

Cost control and reporting is an essential business practice. The visibility that cost control and reporting provides is necessary if you are to respond to potential overruns. Every project manager should get into the habit of establishing an initial project budget, monitoring costs, and analyzing the results. He or she must respond to potential overruns by adjusting work loads, avoiding unnecessary costs, and enlisting the help of those working on the project. Finally, it is necessary to see that the customers live up to their end of the contract by being restricted to what they have paid for and by complying with established schedules.

REVIEW QUESTIONS

1. State some reasons for establishing a project budget and schedule.

2. Develop your own project *spread-sheet* for a five-month, $10,000 project and show what it looks like if the project is completed in four months and final project costs amount to $15,000.

3. Describe two general types of cost collection systems.

4. Why is timeliness a key factor in cost reporting?

5. What is meant by *labor effort type*?

6. Develop your own monthly project cost forecasting form like the one shown in Figure 7-2 using the project spread-sheet data developed in review question 2.

7. Describe some benefits of financial review.

8. How can project cost data affect existing cost standards?

9. What effect does the *learning curve* have on cost standards?

10. What is meant by *customer cost control*?

8

Publications Quality Control Provisions

THE NEED FOR QUALITY CONTROL

To be useful, many kinds of equipment demand good operation and maintenance manuals. For example, many home appliances require operating booklets that are easily read and understood by the home appliance consumer. Good operation and maintenance instructions are of particular importance to operators of complex technical devices, such as computers or air traffic control radar systems. Erroneous information can be hazardous in the case of air traffic control equipment, where ranges, azimuth, and elevation data must be precise and easily understood. Minor errors or sloppy presentation could result in a midair collision.

In those markets where price competition is fierce, such as in home appliances and small-business and personal computing, the cost of maintaining a customer service staff is unthinkable. Companies in these industries are becoming more dependent than ever on good support documentation to make their products useful to the consumer. The product itself may be the best in the world; without a good instruction manual, however, the buyer may believe it to be useless.

Even when an instruction manual is good in presentation, if there are minor mistakes or oversights, the book's credibility will be blunted. Minor errors will cause the user's opinion, relative to product value, to be negative. Therefore, it is essential that steps are taken to assure the quality of a book from a presentation, readability, content adequacy, and technical accuracy points of view. Provisions for publications quality control are presented in this chapter.

PUBLICATIONS QUALITY CONTROL

Many areas must be addressed when considering publications quality control. These include

- Presentation
- Readability
- Content adequacy
- Content accuracy

Each of these is introduced in the following paragraphs. Once introduced, publications' quality assurance techniques are described in the last section of this chapter.

Presentation

Publications presentation is normally controlled by having a designated content specification and style guide. Without these valuable tools, there is no way of knowing publication organization or form. This is particularly important for projects that require the services of several writers. Without good guidelines, each writer will have a tendency to "improvise" as he or she works through the project. The result will be chaos.

Another important benefit of having an established content specification and style guide is that it is possible to obtain customer agreement relative to presentation before the project is begun. If the customer reviews the specifications and agrees to them, there will be no excuse for major deviations once the books are ready for final review.

Content presentation and style presentation are both described in the remainder of this section.

Content Presentation. A detail specification should exist to govern content presentation, which establishes publication organization and depth of coverage. Publication organization involves content outline, which establishes chapters, paragraphs, front matter, and so on. Once the outline is known, the next question to answer involves depth of coverage. Will the subject be skimmed with an overview, or will a detailed description and illustrations down to the "nuts and bolts" be presented? Once these questions are answered, the writing staff knows what is needed relative to content and detail.

Style Presentation.   How are the chapters and paragraphs to be numbered? The next question is one of style. Who is going to read the book, and how should the text read? Style guides include paragraph, figure, and table conventions. They also establish referencing methods. For example, should the word "figure" begin with a capital "F" or a lowercase "f." Should "as shown in Figure 3" or "See figure 3." be used? These are some of the simple questions that a good style guide resolves. The major issue is consistency with an agreed-upon standard. If the project writers follow an established standard, their job will be easier and the customer will know what to expect.

Readability

Readability involves the level at which text is to be written. Readability, which is expressed in "grade level," should match the reading audience. If it is too difficult, comprehension will be minimized. If it is too simple, the text may lose the reader's interest. Advertising copy is usually written at an eighth-grade level. Articles in the *Reader's Digest* also score in this area; grade 8 is considered to be most appropriate for general readership.

The readability level is often established in the project specification or style guide. Several readability indexes may be used, which typically count such things as average sentence length and multisyllabic words. The following procedure can be followed to measure readability:

1. Find the average number of words in 10 sentences in a randomly selected passage of text.
2. Find the number of words that have three syllables or more in a 100-word passage.

3. Obtain the readability score by adding the numbers derived in steps 1 and 2 and multiplying the result by 0.4.

A score of 12 or less is normally considered readable.

There are also graphs, such as the Fry Graph, that are used to determine readability. The Fry Graph, which was published in an article entitled "Readability Formula That Saves Time," in the April 1968 issue of the *Journal of Reading*, requires that the following procedure be used.

1. Randomly select a 100-word passage.
2. Count the number of sentences in the passage.
3. Count the total number of syllables in the passage.
4. Enter the figures on the designated axis of the graph.
5. Determine the area of intersection to derive the "grade" level.

The graph used resembles the one shown in Figure 8-1. Of course, the level of difficulty can also be influenced by the subject matter, reader interest, semantics, and other variables.

Content Adequacy

Content adequacy addresses how thoroughly a subject is covered, relative to the publication's use. If the book is intended to be introductory, adequacy may verify the presence of important topics. If the book is a detail service manual, such as *How to Overhaul Your Chain Saw*, it is important to ensure that lists of required tools, materials, and equipment, procedures covering disassembly, overhaul, reassembly, testing, and troubleshooting, and supporting illustrations and tables are present.

Here again, the publications specification is used as a guideline. Specifications are normally written to assure that a minimum level of information is hurdled. The specification and the book should be laid side by side; each chapter, section, and paragraph should be present. If the specification calls for

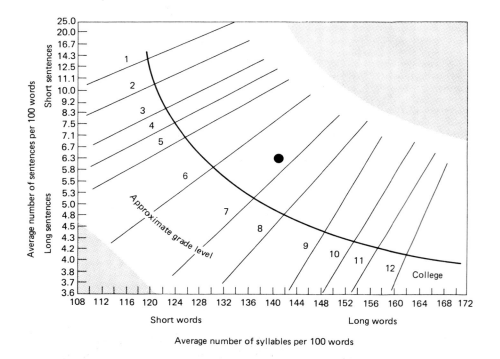

Average number of syllables per 100 words

FIGURE 8-1 **The Fry Readability Graph**

front matter, indexes, and tables, the reviewer should also see that they are present in the proper location and form. Once the reviewer is satisfied that all required information is present, it is time to move on to content accuracy.

Content Accuracy

Content accuracy is essential when the publication product can affect product operation or maintenance or when procedures can affect health or safety. If the information is inaccurate, misleading, ambiguous, or missing, the user may find the product unusable or may wind up with an injury, depending on the product. Those responsible for performing publications reviews go to great lengths to ensure that the product documentation is 100 percent correct. This is done in many ways, which are described in the next section of this chapter.

PUBLICATIONS QUALITY ASSURANCE PROCESSES

Publications quality assurance processes have been established over the years to guarantee that product documentation is presented properly, is readable, is adequate, and is accurate. The processes used for publications reviews include

- In-process reviews
- Subject matter expert reviews
- Validation
- Verification
- Field (beta) testing
- Prepublications reviews
- Customer feedback

Each of these techniques is described in the following paragraphs. Figure 8-2 diagrams the publications quality assurance process.

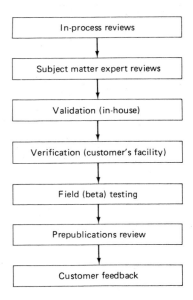

FIGURE 8-2   The Publications Quality Assurance Process

In-Process Reviews

In-process reviews are conducted to assure that the project writing team is "on track." Every publications contractor should welcome the opportunity to participate in an in-process review. First, these reviews ensure that everyone involved in the project has a clear understanding of what is required. This can save a considerable amount of rework resulting from misinterpretation of the requirements. Also, customer representatives can provide guidance as to what they expect to see in the final product and clarify questions that members of the writing staff may have.

Often, deviations to the governing specification are required to handle special situations. These may be requested by either party, the customer or the supplier. Verbal authorization for deviations can be obtained from the customer or contractor representatives during the in-process review meeting. Of course, written confirmation must be received, with the proper approval signatures, if the deviations are to become part of the written contractual documentation.

The number of in-process reviews can vary from one to several, depending on the size of effort and the length of time required to complete it. Often, contracts call for in-process reviews at points of completion. For example, the first might be held at 20 percent completion, the second at 40 percent, a third at 60 percent, and a final in-process review at 80 percent. In-process reviews are normally conducted at the contractor's facility, because source material is more available. However, some contracts alternate the meetings from customer to contractor facility to reduce the burden of travel cost on either party.

Whatever the schedule or travel arrangements, in-process reviews are considered vital to both parties. There are instances, however, when contractors decide that too many in-process reviews can become a burden. This can be true if excessive reviews impede progress and substantially increase labor hours. When the contractor decides this to be the case, a cost factor and schedule slip can be added to accommodate the burden of excessive reviews.

Subject Matter Expert Reviews

As major sections of the book are completed, it is helpful to have subject matter experts review the material for accuracy and adequacy. You will normally find that several subject matter experts will become involved in the review effort. In fact, some writers find that the people who were reluctant to provide source material are the first to jump in with criticism. Many writers are offended by this; others adopt a more philosophical view, thinking of this as a "tricky way" to get inputs from uncooperative resource people.

The number of subject matter reviewers sometimes gets cumbersome.The "too many cooks spoil the broth" routine can easily materialize. This requires that the lead project writer get some agreement from the review team as to specifically who will be the reviewer and when the reviewed material will be returned.

Often, writers find themselves buried in the middle of conflict, finding that two subject matter experts disagree as to what is correct. When this is the case, the writer should normally avoid stepping in and taking sides. Let the subject matter experts find a compromise or have one authoritative subject matter expert who is designated to make all final decisions relative to technical accuracy.

The subject matter expert review is a valuable phase of publications quality assurance. It gives the experts an opportunity to see how their inputs have been interpreted, and to see if what they believe to be true was adequately expressed. Once their comments have been incorporated into a final manuscript, they should be given the opportunity to verify that their critique was properly interpreted. Once this has been done, a final sign-off should be obtained and kept in the project records.

Validation

When contractor personnel take an unreleased book and go through its contents to confirm information adequacy and technical accuracy, the process is called "validation." When the same process is performed by customer personnel, the process is called "verification." The validation process usually involves a responsible writer, either a technical person or a subject matter expert (or both), and an inspector from the contractor's quality assurance organization.

The goal of the validation process is to go through all material in the book to "validate" its suitability for use in the user environment. The writer records changes by marking up a draft copy of the book. The technical members of the validation team perform procedures in the book, trying to simulate the end user's point of view, and the quality inspector certifies that the validation procedure has been accomplished, usually in writing.

When equipment is unavailable to the validation team, they perform what is sometimes referred to as a "desk check." In other words, the team goes through the material without actually performing operating and maintenance procedures but reading them and performing a "dry run." This process is not recommended, particularly for complex technical material. Unfortunately, equipment availability and tight schedules sometimes force the desk check approach to validation. Once the validation process is complete, the writer incorporates all changes in the draft, makes copies, and prepares for the verification process.

Verification

As mentioned, the verification process occurs when a team of customer personnel go through a publication to "verify" information adequacy and accuracy. This process, often referred to as a "verification conference," involves representatives from the contractor, such as a writer and subject matter expert (usually an engineer). The customer is represented by a team of people who will go through the material in a step-by-step fashion. Normally, actual users are enlisted to help. They take a copy of the draft, which includes both text and illustrations, and perform all procedures.

When changes are needed, the writer marks up a master copy of the draft. The subject matter expert serves in an advisory capacity, helping to resolve the need for changes and ensuring that any changes made will not affect the performance or reliability of the involved product.

Once the verification process is complete, minutes of the conference are written and are signed by representatives from both the contractor and customer. The minutes generally include a list of all changes and a copy of the marked-up draft. This material is taken back to the contractor's facility, where it is used to produce the final version of the publication.

Beta (Field) Testing

The validation and verification processes are normally required by large customers, such as governmental agencies or large companies. When a product is being built as a consumer item, the customer does not invoke a contract on the manufacturer containing quality assurance provisions for user documentation. This may be unfortunate, as many publications are little more than merchandising literature with a dearth of helpful product information. However, responsible consumer product manufacturers are sensitive to the need for good documentation and use in-house validation and beta testing.

A beta test consists of selecting a potential product user and supplying that user with the product and supporting publications for some established period of time. This places the product in an actual field environment so that operational performance can be verified. The user records product and documentation deficiencies, which are fed back to the manufacturer and are used to "fine-tune" product performance and supporting publications.

Beta testing can be time consuming, but time helps to uncover those hidden "bugs." An alternative to beta testing is to let the ultimate consumer perform beta testing. This is a tough way to verify quality and could potentially wind up with outraged consumers and lawsuits.

Prepublication Review

The prepublication review is performed just prior to printing. This review is designed to certify that the book is truly ready for printing and distribution. First, it ensures that all validation, verification, or beta test comments, or all three, have been received and are incorporated into the book. Second, it assures that the book has been typeset and laid out in accordance with prevailing specifications and that the camera-ready reproducible copy is suitable for production of negatives or printing plates, or both — depending on the print process to be used.

Once these things have been checked, the inspector, who may be either a customer representative or an in-house quality control inspector, certifies that the publication is ready for production.

Customer Feedback

Another important source of information is customer feedback. To encourage changes, change sheets or tear-out, self-addressed customer comment cards are often included in the back of product instruction books to encourage customer suggestions. The people who use the product often uncover bugs or have valuable suggestions that can be used to improve the quality of the documentation. If comments are received about passages of text that are misunderstood because they are unclear or ambiguous, the documentation should be changed.

Changes cannot be taken lightly. There may be $100,000 worth of book in inventory that could be reprinted because of a small, but important, change. Chapter 9 digs into change control and may have some valuable suggestion to avoid being stuck with a warehouse filled with scrap books.

REVIEW QUESTIONS

1. How can poor-quality documentation affect product acceptance by the end user?

2. What are four primary areas of publication quality control?

3. What document should be used to establish presentation conventions?

4. How is readability expressed? Name two guides used to establish readability levels.

5. What is meant by *content adequacy*?

6. What is the purpose of an *in-process review*?

7. What is the difference between publication *validation* and *verifications*?

8. Describe beta testing.

9. What is the purpose of a prepublication review?

10. How can customer feedback be encouraged?

9

Publications Production

INTRODUCTION

The "front-end" activities of a publications project have been described, including research, cost estimating, contract negotiations, planning and cost tracking, and quality assurance provisions. Once these activities are complete, the book should be ready for final production. This chapter describes the publications production processes with which every professional writer should be familiar. Figure 9-1 charts the path that a typical publication goes through when it is produced. Each section of this chapter describes the elements in the chart.

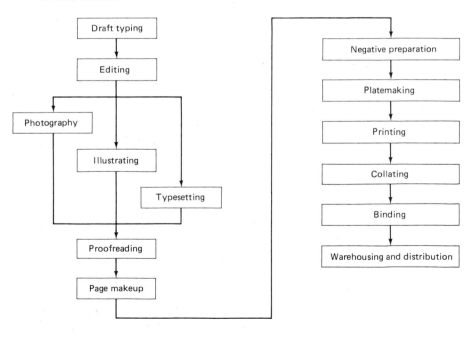

FIGURE 9-1   The Publications Production Process

DRAFT TYPING

The draft typing phase may be optional, depending on the writer's ability to type manuscript and the need for draft typing assistance in incorporating review comments. When word processing equipment is used by both writers and draft typists, it is possible for a draft typist to use the word processor's insert, delete, and move features to incorporate changes to a book that is stored on magnetic media, such as disk or tape. There are installations where the word processor is capable of transferring stored text directly to typesetting equipment, thereby eliminating the need to retype the entire book for typesetting. This process is discussed in more detail in Chapter 11.

The key to having a draft copy is legibility. A clean draft of the publication manuscript is used for review, and in conventional publishing operations, the draft serves as a hard copy input to the production activity.

EDITING

The editing task is extremely important because it is the last in-depth quality checkpoint prior to final production. The editing function includes a grammatical check of the text and verification that approved style, paragraph subordination, and numbering conventions are followed. The editor is also responsible for seeing that illustrations and tables are conveniently located for the reader's use. Finally, the editor must review the draft to ensure that it complies with governing specifications and style guides.

The grammatical edit reviews sentence structure, word usage, and punctuation. Editors ensure that the text and tabular material are written in a clear, concise manner and that terminology is consistent throughout the book. Illustrations are also reviewed to ensure that they are complete, and relate clearly to the text.

The editor also sees that the text is properly marked in preparation for typesetting. Paragraph headings must be designated relative to type size and weight, placement, and line spacing above and below. All paragraphs, illustrations, and tables must be numbered in accordance with prevailing guidelines, and front and back matter must be properly organized and marked.

The editor also finds all references to illustrations and tables. The reference method is checked for consistency, and the text is marked to ensure that text and corresponding illustrations are on the same or facing pages whenever possible.

Another service performed by the editor is to ensure that all unclear passages are queried. When a passage is not clear, it is the editor's responsibility to ask the author of the material for clarification. Once the editorial comments are complete, the marked-up draft is returned to the responsible writer to verify that editorial comments have not altered the meaning of the text.

PHOTOGRAPHY

The responsible writer is normally in charge of obtaining those photographs needed in the book. This is accomplished by scheduling a photographic shooting session with a professional photographer and arranging to have the subject matter available. Many large companies have in-house photographic services. Smaller ones employ the services of local studios.

Preparation

The responsible writer should see that the photographer is supplied with a detailed list of what is needed. Subject matter, views, and lighting conditions (flat or contrast) should be clearly communicated. It is often helpful to provide a descriptive list and sketches of what you are after. In addition to the studio work, the writer should also specify number of prints by size and finish. Common sizes are 3½" × 5", 5"× 7", 8" × 10", and 11" × 14". Finishes are matte and glossy. The matte is often preferred because it is easier to write on.

Studio Photography

When the photographs are of equipment, the pictures should be taken in a studio whenever possible. This helps to assure that lighting can be properly controlled for best results. Glare, or "hot spots," harsh shadow, reflection, and many other factors must be controlled. Where color is used, the light temperature is an important consideration.

Location Photography

If the shooting must be done on location, the photographer should be equipped with a good set of portable lights, lens filters, and sometimes rolled paper for backdrop and foreground use. Portable lights, although not as controllable as those in a professional studio, are often essential in the production of acceptable quality photographs. The lens filters must often be used to compensate for ambient lighting conditions. For example, color lens filters are required when shooting color film under fluorescent light to eliminate the common green cast caused by this type of lighting. Foreground and background paper is often necessary for reflection or to hide unattractive clutter in the area.

Final Photographs

Final photographs are usually pasted in place by either the art department or the page makeup function. They must be "sized," which requires that the photographer use an enlarger to make the subject a specific dimension. This is done to make the photograph fit in an available space. Once the photographs are sized and are pasted in place, they are incorporated into the book's camera-ready reproducible art package, which is what goes to the printing preparation area.

Here, high-contrast screened negatives or screened prints are made in preparation for print reproduction. Notice the term *high contrast*; film used for film preparation, called *photolithographic negatives*, is either black or white. The film used for making photographs is called *continuous tone* film, which has tonal values ranging from white, to all shades of gray, to black. The photolithographic film process is described in more detail in the section on negative preparation.

ILLUSTRATING

The writer must also work closely with the illustrating function, where artwork and mechanically drawn diagrams are prepared for inclusion in the book. As with photographs, it is important to provide a detailed list of all required illustrations in addition to sketches and supporting engineering drawings and photographs.

Sizing

It is also important to specify the size needed for each piece of art so that it can be placed in the proper location in the book. It is desirable to avoid "foldout" pages, that must be unfolded by the reader. The goal should be to keep everything on standard-sized pages. Whenever possible, artwork should be oriented in the same position as text. There are times when the shape and size of artwork causes it to be placed sideways. This is called a *turn* or *tip page*. Again, it is common practice to avoid turn pages whenever possible.

Line and Tone Art

When the illustrator prepares a drawing with pen and ink, black tape, and "rub-down" art, the resulting illustration is called *line art*. In contrast, photographic illustrations are referred to as *tone art*.

Illustration Lettering

Where engineering diagrams are used, lettering is usually done by mechanical means. Often, the illustrator draws all lines and symbols, and the lettering is done by a typist using a special, wide carriage or open-ended type-writer. Another commonly used technique is to type all required lettering on adhesive-backed stock. The illustrator then cuts out the strips of lettering and "sticks" them in place.

TYPESETTING

Typesetting is the process used to prepare camera-ready text. The equipment used to prepare typeset-quality text varies. As late as the 1950s, typesetting was accomplished on "hot lead" machines, which molded a reverse image of each character in lead. The characters were aligned and mounted on letter-press equipment, where the page was printed directly from the type. Since that time, new approaches to typesetting have been developed. These include direct impression typesetting, photocomposition, and laser printer composition.

Direct-Impression Typesetting

In the 1960s, direct-impression typesetting became popular. This process, once referred to as a "cold type" to differentiate from the more common "hot-type" process that used molten lead, was similar to typewriting. Equipment such as IBM Selectric composers, which offer type sizes ranging from 6 to 12 points in a number of styles, is used for direct impression typesetting. This equipment is still in use today, although it is no longer considered to be "state-of-the-art" type composition.

Photocomposition

Photocomposition equipment is being used more and more in recent years for typesetting. There are two general types of photocomposers. The early- technology photocomposition equipment uses negative filmstrips on which type is contained. To provide a range of type styles from which to choose without changing filmstrips, film-based photocomposers store from 4 to 16 selectable type faces on line, depending on the manufacturer.

When a character is to be set, a beam of light passes through the selected character, it is magnified by a lens system for size, and the character image is focused on photographic positive paper. Hence the term "photocomposition." The photo paper must be developed before it can be exposed to light and pasted in place as text.

Another kind of typesetter uses digital representations of character images stored on magnetic media rather than on filmstrips. These systems, which use computer technology, are much faster than the film-type photocomposers and typically store from 20 to 250 selectable typefaces on line.

Laser Composition

Laser composition devices, which are emerging, use laser printing technology in place of the photographic process. The laser process focuses the type image on a rotating drum. The latent image picks up a toner mixture, which is transferred to paper. The process is similar to the Xerographic process used in bond copiers. Type images are stored in a manner similar to digitized photocomposition machines.

The advantage to laser printing is that it places high-quality type directly on dry paper. This eliminates the need for developing positive film, saving time and the cost of photoprocessing equipment.

Typesetting Advantages

Typeset text has many advantages over typewritten text. First, the text is more attractive. Second, it is condensed relative to typewritten text, allowing more information to be placed on fewer pages. This advantage reduces production costs, because there are fewer pages, negatives, and printing plates. In addition, the publications will be lighter, reducing storage, handling, and shipping costs.

A third advantage of typeset material is that it is actually easier to read. More words can be packed on each line, which minimizes the left-to-right eye movement. It is commonly agreed that short text lines are physically easier to read than are long text lines.

Typesetting Codes

Typesetters require type command codes to be embedded in text. These codes instruct the typesetter to select type sizes, styles, line lengths, vertical space between lines, called *leading*, and other commands for centering text, ruling it, and *kerning*. Kerning is a term used for modifying intercharacter spacing. Characters can be overlapped or spread apart depending on the desired effect.

When text is entered on the typesetter from typewritten draft, the operator must refer to a type specification that provides type and layout guidelines. In addition to typing the text, the proper codes must also be typed. When text already exists in a form that can be stored in the typesetter from either a computer or word processor database, the typesetter operator need only insert the command codes. This saves a significant amount of keyboard time and minimizes the potential for typographical errors.

Some word processor to typesetter networks allow the codes to be embedded on the word processor. Because word processor text editors are normally more functional than are those on typesetters, many companies are finding that their word processors are much more efficient typesetter "front ends" than is the typesetter keyboard itself. This arrangement is discussed in more detail in Chapter 11.

Type Formatters

Some computer-based type formatter programs are designed to convert text files into typeset output. These programs typically feature menus, or lists of questions about type styles, line lengths, and page depths. Abbreviated codes are placed in the text to identify headings and items that require special treatment. The formatter program converts these to a set of more complex codes used by the typesetter. In addition, formatter programs can automatically adjust the number of lines per page, eliminate widows, and insert such things as running heads, footers, and page numbers.

Type Output

Type normally comes out of a typesetter in what is called "galley" form. Galley is a running strip of paper on which the type is set. The galley is normally proofread to ensure that it is in the proper form and that typographical errors have not been made. Once proofread and corrected, the type is next given to the page makeup function. The following two sections describe proofreading and page makeup.

PROOFREADING

The proofreading phase of production is important to assure that the final typeset material accurately reflects the manuscript. Proofreading verifies that the final typeset material, commonly referred to as "repro" (reproducible copy), is a character-for-character, word-for-word copy of the manuscript. Typographical errors and omissions are marked using standard proofreading marks. The repro is returned to the typesetting function where all proofreading marks are reviewed and incorporated. Often, the responsible editor also reviews the proofread material to ensure that the style has not been affected.

PAGE MAKEUP

Once all corrections have been made and the final typeset text and artwork are available, the book is pasted up in pages. Most often, the pages are mounted on heavy paper stock, referred to as *board art*, which keeps it from being wrinkled. The type is laid down on the board art, along with running heads, footers, and page numbers. Line art is normally mounted in place; solid black or red *knock-out blocks* are frequently placed in the area where tone art will be used. If screened prints are used instead of *halftone negatives*, which will be described in the next section of this chapter, they are sometimes pasted in place.

The final product of the page makeup function is camera-ready reproducible copy. Once the repro package is complete, it is usually given one more inspection by the writer and editor. If the publication is prepared under a contract that requires a prepublications review, this is when a customer inspector will inspect the material.

Camera-ready repro is rarely let out of the production area. It is considered the culmination of months of hard labor and represents a major investment. If a review is to be performed out of the area, copies are used. Even when reviews are made in the production area, reviewers are cautioned not to mark on the repro. They are encouraged to use separate sheets of paper for their comments. Once all review comments are resolved and the repro is ready for printing, it is common to have the responsible program manager sign a Release for Publication form.

The repro package is now ready for the printing process. The package is often accompanied by a Reproduction Assembly Sheet, which is usually prepared by the responsible editor, and contains an inventory of all pages. The sheet shows which pages are to be printed two sides and which ones have blank backs. The sheet also tells the printer where line and tone art will appear. The printer uses the Reproduction Assembly Sheet for job planning and layout.

Once approval is received, the book is ready for printing, where its first stop will be the "prep area," where photo negatives of each page are made.

NEGATIVE PREPARATION

Unless direct-image printing plates are used, the first stage in the printing process is the production of high-contrast film negatives of each page. This is the source of the term "camera ready." Negatives are made using a large *process camera.* Figure 9-2 shows a diagram of such a camera.

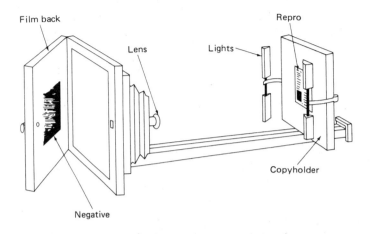

FIGURE 9-2   The Process Camera

The Process Camera

The repro page is placed on a lighted copyholder, and a page-sized negative is produced. Depending on the size of the camera, this is done a page at a time, or it can be "gang shot" producing several pages at a time. Most lithographic cameras, which are located in a dark room except for the copyholder, have large film backs which swing open like a door. The film, emulsion side toward the copyholder, is laid flat on the film back. The copyholder lights are turned on, the camera's lens is opened, and the negative is exposed.

When the film is removed and developed, the white areas of the repro page become solid black on the film; the black images on the page, including text and line work, are clear.

Halftone Production

When tone art (continuous tone photographs) is supplied with the repro package, halftone negatives must be prepared. This is done by using a *screen*, which is an opaque film sheet with rows (or lines) of clear round dots. The dots are small, typically ranging from 85 to 133 per inch. The screen is laid over the undeveloped film on the film back, and the light that is reflected from the repro page to the film passes through the dots. The result is that the latent image of the photograph becomes a series of black dots. White areas of the repro page are solid, because high-intensity exposure areas cause the dots to overlap. Gray and black tones leave the dots smaller, and the dot grain can be seen.

When "screened prints" are used as original art in the repro package, they are shot as line negatives. Screened prints are made from black dots and can be copied directly using the high-contrast lithographic film. Generally, better quality photo reductions can be obtained by using the halftone negative rather than by making line shots of existing screened prints. The line shot of an existing screened print is a second-generation reproduction, where the screened negative process gets closer to the original photograph.

Stripping

The negatives are next mounted on large opaque sheets. The page image area is cut out of the sheets so that the clear areas of the film will be unobstructed during the platemaking process. The negatives may be mounted one to a sheet, 4-up, 8-up, or 16-up, depending upon the size of the printing press to be used. One-up is used for small offset duplicators, which commonly run in a 12" × 18" maximum sheet size. When larger presses are used, several pages may be mounted together allowing several to be printed simultaneously. This is called a *signature*. Signatures are consecutive pages in a book, and they must be accurately registered and checked to see that each page is in the proper location within the signature.

When the negatives are stripped in place, they are laid on light tables. "Pinholes," scratches, and "cut lines," which result from edge shadows on pasted up repro, must be opaqued, using a special opaque fluid and brushes or opaque markers. Once all white areas are completely opaque, and text and line work are clear (transparent), the negatives are ready to be used for making printing plates.

PLATEMAKING

There are many kinds of plates. Some are of the direct-image type, which eliminate the need to go through the negative process. However, these are normally lower quality and have a shorter run life. We will briefly discuss some of the direct-image types of platemakers; then we will discuss the use of film in platemaking.

Direct-Image Platemakers

The simplest type of direct-image plate can be prepared directly on a typewriter. An image of the typewritten character is pressed onto a carrier sheet. The image, which is reversed and resembles a carbon copy, can be mounted directly on a small offset press. The carbonlike deposit carries the ink in the printing press, while the rest of the sheet retards the ink.

Inexpensive electrostatic platemakers are also used in short-run, small offset press shops. The equipment used to produce electrostatic plates resembles small office copiers, where the repro page is simply laid on a glass copyholder and a light source "sweeps" the repro, placing a latent toner image of the repro page on a transfer drum. The latent image is fused to the plate material with heat. The toner serves as a carrier for the ink.

Other direct-image processes use plasticized-paper and mylar-based plate material. These systems resemble small, upright process cameras. The repro is placed on a copyholder and is photographed on photosensitive plate material. These systems feature a complete plate developing and drying circuit. The photosensitive plate material is rollfed, and each plate is cut from the roll and transported through the developing process.

Conventional Platemaking

The film-to-metal plate process is still the most commonly used by large printing plants. Metal plates hold up for millions of printed impressions and are considered reliable. The metal plate is made by exposing an emulsion surface to high-intensity light through a film negative. Figure 9-3 is a diagram of this process. Once the plate is exposed through the negative, it is developed. The latent image is developed emulsion, which carries ink. The unexposed areas wipe clean and retard ink.

The developing process is performed in the light. Developer can be applied to the metal plate by wiping it on with a rag or squeegie. There are also plate developing machines that pull the plate through with a roller system. Applicator strips apply the developing solutions and wipe

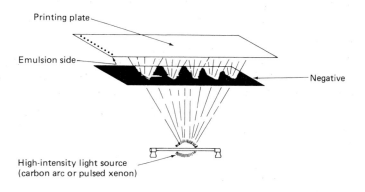

FIGURE 9-3 Plate Exposure Diagram

them off. The plate comes out of these machines clean and is ready to be mounted on the printing press.

PRINTING

Now that the plates are made, the book is ready for printing. Here, we will discuss offset printing rather than "letter press" printing, which still has some limited use.

The Offset Printing Process

The offset printing process uses ink and water "fountains," which are nothing more than trays, and a roller system to mix the ink and water in the proper ratio. The watered ink becomes emulsified and is transported by another set of rollers to the master cylinder, where the plate is attached. The ink adheres to the emulsion on the rotating plate. An impression cylinder, which is covered by a rubberlike *blanket*, presses against the rotating master cylinder. The ink is transferred, or "offset," from the plate to the blanket. Next, paper is fed between the impression cylinder's blanket and a chrome roller, and the ink is offset from the blanket to the paper. The paper is passed to a delivery tray in the form of a printed page.

Setup Time versus Press Runtime

As each new plate is installed on the press, the blanket must be thoroughly cleaned with "blanket wash," which is a high-grade kerosene. Once a new plate is installed, it must be properly registered on the page. These steps take time, and are all part of what is called "setup time."

If a relatively small number of printed copies is required for each plate, such as 25 or 50, the job is considered "short run." The ratio of setup time to "press run time" is higher for short-run jobs than for those that are classified as "long run." This increases the unit cost of each printed page. On the other hand, if the job is long run, such as 25,000 copies of each plate, the setup time will be low relative to press run time. Both setup time and press run time must be considered when scheduling and cost estimating the printing task.

COLLATING

When all pages have been printed, they must be collated in the proper order in preparation for final book binding. The collating process involves gathering all pages into book sets, ensuring that they are in the proper order. There are several different types of collating equipment. They range from small, hand-fed units to high-volume, automated machines that are used to process large, long-run book production.

Sorters

A sorter is predominantly used in short-run, sheet-fed printing operations, where each sheet is gathered in a separate bin as it comes off the press. In this way, each bin contains a separate book, or section of a book, depending on the bin capacity. By printing the last page first, it will lie on the bottom of the stack. The next-to-last page is printed second and so on until the last page printed is page one, which winds up on top of the stack in each bin. The number of books that can be gathered is limited by the number of bins in a sorter. They are commonly available in multiples of 50, and many units are available with 200 bins.

Sorters are often run on line; that is, the press feeds the printed pages directly into the sorter so that collated documents come directly from the press room. Sorters can also be used off line. Pages come from the press room in individual stacks. The collating function uses a sheet feeder to deliver each page to the sorter, and each stack of pages must be processed.

Collators

Collators are common to sheet-fed operations that have medium to long print runs. Collators differ from sorters in that printed page sets are placed in bins in the proper order, one sheet is gathered from each bin and is collated with the other sheets, and the resulting pile of paper is stacked at the output end of the collator in sets.

Collators differ from sorters in that they typically have between 10 and 50 bins, but the bins are larger and collators typically have fewer bins, ranging from 10 to 50, but the bins are larger, allowing several hundred sheets to be stored in each one. Some collators handle 11"×17" paper stock and are equipped with wire stitching (staple) equipment, allowing books to be automatically "saddle-stitched" as they are delivered from the gathering mechanism.

Signature Collating

Where large sheet-fed or roll-fed (web) presses are used, and multiple pages are printed in a single pass, the pages must be separated in the proper order. If a press prints a signature of 16 pages on a single sheet of paper. the sheet is folded in such a way as to allow all pages to be in the proper order. Once the signature sheet is folded, the edges are trimmed. This results in having 16 sheets of paper, or pages.

Large automated folders and trimmers perform the signature collating process. This equipment is used extensively in high-volume printing operations.

BINDING

Once the document is collated into the proper order, the next step is binding. There are many methods used to bind books. We will briefly discuss several methods that are commonly used. These include

- Wire stitching (corner, side, and saddle)
- Plastic comb binding
- Spiral wire binding
- Post binding
- Perfect binding
- Case binding

Wire Stitching

A wire stitch is actually nothing more than a staple, although many types of bindery staplers use roll wire to form the staple as it is used. A corner stitch is simply a staple in the upper left-hand corner of the document. Corner stitching is normally used to hold the pages together in a set. Often, corner stitched documents are three-hole drilled to allow the book to be placed in standard three-ring notebook binders.

When side stitching is used, two or three staples are placed along the left side of the document, about 3/16" to 5/16" from the binding edge. A saddle stitch is used when a book is folded in the center, and two or three staples are pressed from the outside folded edge through to the inside center fold. This method is used for small books that are normally less than 80 pages (20 sheets of paper).

Wire stitching is among the most economical ways to bind books. It is fast, the material is inexpensive, and the equipment used for wire stitching is among the least expensive.

Plastic Comb Binding

Plastic comb binding, sometimes referred to as Cerlox® or GBC binding, is another popular method, which uses a 19-ring plastic spine that wraps through rectangular holes that are punched along the binding edge of the book. (Cerlox is a trademark of General Binding Corporation.) The plastic spines come in different sizes ranging from around one-fourth of an inch to a few inches. A plastic bound book normally lays open or folds back, making it easy to read.

Plastic binding requires more manual labor than do the stitching methods of binding. The labor is expended in hole punching and spine insertion. The material for plastic binding is relatively inexpensive, usually under 50 cents per unit, and the equipment can be purchased for under $2,500.

Spiral Wire Binding

Wire binding is an attractive and durable binding technique. A major advantage of this binding method is that the book can be laid flat or folded over. Many users like this technique relative to other alternatives. When first introduced, it was more expensive than plastic binding. However, automation techniques are making it more economical. In some parts of the United States, spiral wire binding is actually less expensive than is plastic binding.

Post Binding

Post binding, which uses aluminum screw posts, requires three-hole drilled paper stock. Screw posts come in different lengths to fit different thicknesses of books. Post binding is highly labor intensive, as each screw must be inserted and tightened by hand. When books are thick, screw posts often make them difficult to read because the book must be forcefully spread to see the inside edge of center pages.

Perfect Binding

Perfect binding is a popular and attractive way to bind books. A typical "pocket book" is a good example of a perfect-bound book. Medium sized printing operations often subcontract perfect binding to companies that specialize in this process.

Perfect-bound books are held together with binding glue. This glue is heated before it is applied to the book. The outside cover, which is creased to fold to the proper size, is wrapped around the book as it is bound. The glue hardens when it cools. Next, the perfect-bound books are trimmed to final size at the top, bottom, and outside edge with a three-knife trimmer. Perfect binding requires a substantial investment in equipment relative to the other binding processes already discussed, but the material cost is low, and the process is more machine intensive, reducing the unit labor cost.

Case Binding

Case-bound books are what most people refer to as "hard-back" books, when compared with perfect-bound books, which are called "soft bound" or "paper back." The cover of a case bound book is made from what people often call "chipboard," which is similar to the gray cardboard material found on the back of writing tablets. The board is wrapped in preprinted paper or fabric, which is glued in position, to form a "wrap-around" cover. Next, the wrap-around cover is glued to the binding edge of the book. Often, the signatures are sewn together with binding thread. This process is called Smythe sewn and provides extra strength to book binding.

To determine whether the Smythe-sewn process has been used, you can look at the top or bottom of a book and see the binding thread "header," which is usually two color.

Also, if you spread the book open, you can see the stitches at the binding edge.

Summary

Each binding process has a place. Print run length, cost, durability, aesthetics, packaging for merchandising appeal, competitive market pressures, and many other factors must be weighed when selecting a method. Once the method is selected, the cost of the binding method must be included in financial forecasts and inventory value.

WAREHOUSING AND DISTRIBUTION

Once books are printed, they are ready to be stored in the warehouse or delivered to the customer. When the book is delivered directly to the customer from the print shop, the headaches of warehousing and distribution are greatly simplified. When it must be stocked and delivered from a warehouse, each copy must be accounted for. In this section, we will describe some of the problems associated with warehousing and distribution from inventory.

Warehousing

Books should be kept in a dry environment. Either the warehouse should be dry, or the books should be placed in boxes to retard humidity. An accurate count of the book's inventory level should also be maintained. Normally, well-managed warehousing operations will have computer-based inventory control systems that reflect exactly how many units are on the shelf for every part number.

These systems also tell management when the stock levels fall below reorder point, so that the inventory can be replenished. Another valuable output of the inventory control system is "stockturn" visibility. If the book is being consumed either above or below expectations, the inventory levels can be adjusted.

All well-managed companies are sensitive to inventory levels, as this is a major cash investment. In addition, inventory levels occupy precious space, are subject to local taxes, and are subject to fire and theft. For these reasons, inventory must be managed at the lowest acceptable level to minimize liability.

Another problem associated with excessive inventory is obsolescence. If a major product modification is made, it is possible that the entire stock will become obsolete. This requires that the inventory is "written off" by the company, which increases operating costs.

When the inventory level is high, and a change is issued, there are times when change packages, discussed in the next chapter, are issued. Each change package must be issued with each copy of the book in stock. The added labor for doing this is an extra expense of doing business.

All these reasons point to the need to minimize inventory levels. The production operation will be pressing for long run, because they realize that the *economy of scale* will yield lower unit cost. On the other hand, those responsible for inventory management will want the amount adjusted downward. In most companies, it is the inventory managers who prevail, because they know what the stock levels should be by having a record of inventory turn.

Distribution

If the book is the final product, it must be packaged properly for shipping. If it is a durably bound book, it may be shipped by simply sticking a mailing label to it and putting it in the mail. Of course, there will likely be some bending of corners and abrasions, but this may not be important in the particular market being served.

Books are heavy; a small quantity may be shipped by mail at a reasonable rate. But it does not take many to require a freight handler. Therefore, most books are shipped over the road. They are subject to rough handling. They can be easily damaged from their own weight if dropped. For this reason, the packing container should be durable. If· the books are going into retail operations, they should arrive in good condition. The containers used should be designed so the books fit tightly. This will prevent the books from being bent or crushed due to sliding around inside a loose carton.

If the book is to be shipped with a product, provisions should be made to include the book in the product packaging. If the product has lubricants or surfaces that can soil or discolor the book, it may be wise to put the book in a paper or plastic envelope or cover it with a "heat-shrink" plastic wrapper.

SUMMARY

A brief overview of production processes has been provided in this chapter. We have followed a book from manuscript to final distribution. Every professional writer should be familiar with these processes so that project planning, cost estimating, and publications program management can be performed more knowledgeably. In the next chapter, publications configuration and change control are discussed. This is another topic that is vital to the professional publications manager.

REVIEW QUESTIONS

1. Which production phase is often the last in-depth quality checkpoint prior to final production?

2. What kind of information should a writer supply to a photographer?

3. What is the difference between *high-contrast* and *continuous tone* photographic film?

4. What is a *turn page*?

5. Name two modern typesetting methods.

6. Why is typeset text preferred to typewritten text?

7. What is meant by the term *repro*?

8. What is a screen (as used in halftone preparation)?

9. What type of printing plate is considered most durable?

10. What is the difference between printing *setup time* and *run time*?

11. What is the difference between a *sorter* and a *collator*?

12. What are other terms for *perfect-bound* and *case-bound* books?

13. Name some problems associated with high inventory levels.

10

Publications Configuration and Change Control

INTRODUCTION

Publications configuration and change control is an important consideration in book design, achieving updates at a minimum cost, warehousing, and distribution. When configuration and change control procedures exist from the beginning, revisions to your publications inventory, to those books that are already in customers' hands, or to both stored and distributed books will not be a major problem. If you have not planned for configuration and change control, you may find yourself in a dilemma: misinformed product users and a warehouse full of worthless paper. In this chapter, configuration and change control techniques are described.

CONFIGURATION CONTROL

The U.S. government and military services have long-standing configuration control procedures that are used by contractors. These procedures require all modifications to equipment to be precisely tracked to ensure compatibility of deployed equipment. As new equipment is produced, it must be interchangeable with existing equipment in "form, fit, and function."

If a variety of configurations exists, spare parts will be rendered useless, operation and maintenance will be made more difficult, training on multiple configurations may become impossible, and all will likely come to a grinding halt.

Needless to say, the ability to provide good supporting publications will also become difficult. Therefore, the responsibility for configuration control begins with the product being described, which is a function of engineering and manufacturing. Good product configuration control procedures ensure that changes are clearly documented and distributed. The changes should be traceable to product type and serial number, and the change information should be distributed to the product support groups, including Publications and Field Service. When change information is documented and distributed, the publications organization must be prepared to incorporate changes into the product support publications.

There are times when changes to the product publications are made to correct content mistakes, omissions, or such things as typographical errors. When this is done, a record of the change should be maintained, and the publication, itself, should be annotated to reflect the change. Information about publications change control techniques and annotation techniques are discussed in the section of this chapter.

PUBLICATIONS CHANGE CONTROL

There are a number of approaches that can be taken to reflect changes in product publications and to distribute the product information to both the warehouse and the field. This section presents several approaches, including

- Configuration control records (effectivity control sheets and annotation)
- Distribution records
- Errata sheets
- Change packages
- Revisions and reissues

Before getting into specific procedures and examples, some definitions are provided:

- *Original issue* — The first edition of a book
- *Errata* — pen and ink corrections to a publication
- *Errata sheet* — instructions that are given to a publication user for making pen and ink corrections
- *Change* — a minor change in a publication

- *Change package* — a set of new pages and an instruction sheet to enable the user to replace old pages with new ones
- *Revision* — a major change to a publication, usually requiring reprint
- *Revision and reissue* — a new edition of a publication that replaces existing issues

Configuration Control Records

There are several things that can be done to trace configuration control throughout the life of a publication. These include the establishment and maintenance of a master history file for each publication, having an up-to-date Effectivity Control Sheet in each of the publications, and marking each page affected by changes.

Master History File. The master history file for each publication should contain all change documentation, including at least one copy of every version of the book, beginning with the original issue. Records of each change, including the reasons, dates, authorizing signatures, and all supporting paperwork, should be maintained. The master history file serves as a source for all changes and provides the information needed to maintain the book's Effectivity Control Sheet.

Effectivity Control Sheet. The Effectivity Control Sheet is normally a page, often located at the inside front cover, that inventories the status of all pages within a book. A typical Effectivity Control Sheet contains information similar to that shown in Figure 10-1. Notice that each page or group of pages is maintained by issue date and change number. The change numbers are listed at the top of the sheet with their corresponding dates. The sheet shows all changes throughout the life of an issue. If the book is reissued, all pages normally carry the reissue date, and the change numbers revert to number 1.

EFFECTIVITY CONTROL SHEET

This publication contains 86 pages that have been altered by the following changes:

Original issue: January 1, 1982
Change 1:   April 15, 1982
Change 2:   October 1, 1982

The effectivity of the pages in this book is tabulated in the following list.

NOTE: Unless otherwise specified, pages are original issue.

Front Cover	Change 2	Section 4	
Title Page	Change 2	Pages 4-1 through 4-12	
Front Matter		Section 5	
Pages ii through iii	Change 2	Page 5-1	Change 2
Pages iv through v	Change 1	Pages 5-2 through 5-3	
Pages vi through x		Pages 5-4 through 5-5	Change 1
Section 1		Pages 5-6 through 5-10	
Pages 1-1 through 1-2	Change 1	Section 6	
Page 1-3	Change 2	Pages 6-1 through 6-10	
Pages 1-4 through 1-6		Pages 6-11 through 6-14	Change 2
Section 2		Pages 6-15 through 6-20	
Pages 2-1 through 2-10		Section 7	
Section 3		Page 7-1	Change 1
Pages 3-1 through 3-3		Pages 7-2 through 7-4	
Page 3-4	Change 2	Page 7-5	Change 2
Pages 3-5 through 3-6		Pages 7-6 through 7-11	

FIGURE 10-1   A Sample Effectivity Control Sheet

Configuration Annotation.   Each page affected by a change normally contains information at the bottom such as

Change 2, October 1, 1983

Within the body of the text, a change bar, which is a heavy vertical line, is normally located along the outside margin of the text or artwork affected by the change. If change bars already exist from a previous change, they are removed. This shows the reader where the changes are located for easy comparison to prior versions of the book.

Distribution Records

When configuration and change control is a major concern, it is important to know where copies are located. Distribution records are established in two general ways. In the case of limited-distribution items, owners or users are registered when the product is initially sold at the point of sale. Mass-distribution items, such as consumer products, require that owners fill out mail-in registration forms contained in the product literature. The distribution records are normally kept in large computer databases so that sorting by configuration or model number and the printing of mailing labels are easily achieved.

Errata Sheets

Errata sheets are a common means of issuing minor changes. An errata sheet package normally includes a cover letter describing the nature of the change and a list of instructions for making pen and ink corrections. The list normally includes very precise markup instructions, such as

> Page 16, second paragraph, third line: Replace "Turn gain control R32 counterclockwise until the volume is at a comfortable level" with "Turn squelch control R36 clockwise until the audio output cuts off."

> Page 32, first paragraph, fourth line: Change the sentence "Press the transmitter button." to "Press and hold the transmitter button."

In publications having Effectivity Control Sheets, the markup instructions normally include entries on what changes should be made on the Effectivity Control Sheet.

Errata sheets are often mailed to registered holders of the affected product publication as well as inserted in those books remaining in inventory. When the book is reprinted, those pages containing errata changes are normally reworked to eliminate the need for customers to make errata changes. The errata sheet is the least expensive way of making changes to existing publications.

Change Packages

Change packages are used to update publications similarly to errata sheets, except that instead of having users make pen and ink corrections, they are requested to replace old pages with new ones. The change package also includes a cover letter and a list of instructions to be sure the user replaces all pages. Normally, the change package will include a new cover page and Effectivity Control Sheet to show the latest changes. As mentioned earlier, all change pages contain the change number and date and often show change bars. Change packages, like errata sheets, are used when only a small percentage of the pages in a book is affected by a change.

The change packages are normally placed in stock and are delivered with each copy of the book when it is pulled from inventory. When a new stock of books is required, the change pages are normally reprinted and collated with the rest of the publication. Of course, change pages continue to carry all change annotation until a revision and reissue takes place.

Revisions And Reissues

A revision and reissue is required when major changes take place or when numerous small changes exist that affect a large percentage of the book's contents. For example, if a change impacts as much as 25 to 30 percent of a book, it should probably be reprinted. The book's publisher should not expect the reader to be inconvenienced performing publication housekeeping tasks.

When a revision and reissue take place, it is nothing more than a new edition. All change pages are converted to reissued pages. Change annotation disappears, and the only evidence of change is that the Effectivity Control Sheet and title page normally state

Original Issue: January 1, 1984
Revised and Reissued: January 1, 1986

A subsequent change becomes Change 1 to the revised and reissued version.

SUMMARY

There are several things to consider when choosing the change method, that is, errata sheet, change package, or revision and reissue. These include

1. The number of books affected, including those distributed and in inventory
2. The cost of errata, change package, or reissue production and distribution
3. The amount of user inconvenience in making an erratum or a change
4. The number of pages affected by a single change or cumulative multiple changes

When these factors are weighed, a better choice can be made.

In situations where changes are frequent, it is advisable to limit the size of the book inventory to be printed. Many manufacturers try to hold the number down to between six months and a year. This prevents manufacturers from having to scrap a large number of books as a result of major product changes or discontinuance and also makes change distribution simpler.

The key, however, is to have an established configuration and change control procedure and a distribution list so that a suitable choice is available. Without an established configuration and change control procedure or distribution list, there may be no choice. This is particularly true in the case of a consumer appliance that has a defect considered to be a safety hazard. If a vehicle for notifying registered owners does not exist, the manufacturer may have to itself "go public" by advertising the defect in national media.

REVIEW QUESTIONS

1. What are some of the consequences associated with having multiple-product configurations?

2. List several approaches used to make changes to existing publications.

3. What should a *master history file* contain?

4. What is the purpose of an *Effectivity Control Sheet*?

5. Which change method should be used to control pen and ink corrections?

6. Describe the contents of a *change package*.

7. When is a *revision and reissue* advisable?

11

Writing, Publications Management, and Publications Production Automation

INTRODUCTION

This chapter looks at some common methods available for automating both writing and publications management tasks. It looks at the evolution of computer systems over the past 20 years. Some ways that word processing, computerized typesetting, financial analysis, database management, and dictation systems can be used in the publications environment are described. All these applications can be used to drive the cost of publications planning, development, and production down, thereby increasing profitability.

COMPUTERS IN PUBLICATIONS

The publications automation process is highly dependent on modern computer systems. Large mainframe systems were the mainstay of publications automation in the 1960s and early 1970s. These systems, which offered relatively crude text editors, document formatters and fast printers, were used by very large companies, because small companies simply could not afford the luxury of a mainframe costing $1,000,000. Accordingly, the small companies had to wait for the price of automation to reach an affordable level.

Minicomputers, which were the next generation of computers, became prominent in the early 1970s. Smaller in size yet still powerful enough to perform most of the tasks needed, they became a viable alternative for many midsized companies. But publications-specific applications software, by today's standards, was still relatively crude. Although there were some exceptions, the electronic data processing emphasis was still on centralized corporate accounting functions.

Distributed systems that supported individual department productivity were still difficult to cost-justify.

Technology continued to push back size and cost, and the microcomputer evolved. In the mid-1970s, microcomputers were an attraction for hobbyists. There was a lack of software standardization and good applications programs, and software developers were still unsure as to which microprocessors would become dominant in the market. The start was sluggish, but once a trend was detected, the software developers rushed in to fill the void of microcomputer software.

An ex-Intel employee named Gary Kildall started a company named Digital Research, which produced the CP/M (control program for microcomputers) operating system for the Intel 8080 and Zylog Z-80 microcomputers. This control program prepared a fertile environment for software developers, and within a few years, a few thousand CP/M-compatible programs existed.

Other "private-label" operating systems were introduced by the growing number of computer and software companies. Apple Computer, which built its computer system around the Rockwell 6502 microprocessor offered Apple DOS (disk operating system.) Tandy-Radio Shack jumped in with its line of Z-80 machines offering a variety of TRS DOS operating systems. Microsoft introduced PC-DOS for the 16-bit IBM Personal Computer and MS-DOS for such machines as the Texas Instruments Professional Computer. These machines, which operate on Intel's 8088 microcomputer, are beginning to take the place of the 8-bit 8080, Z-80 machines.

But these are only a beginning. The performance-price curve continues to be driven down by technological advances in both hardware and software. At this writing, a wave of even faster, more versatile Motorola MC68000 microcomputer-based machines are being produced and are predicted to dominate the microcomputer industry in the late 1980s. So the push goes on. From mainframe to mini to micro, and from 8-bit to 16-bit to 32-bit. Computers more powerful than those that 20 years ago required several floors of a building and tons of air conditioning equipment now fit in a briefcase. And, just as remarkable, these tiny marvels cost a fraction of the cost.

SYSTEM SELECTION

We will be looking at microcomputers in the balance of this chapter. First, microcomputers are within financial reach of even the smallest companies. Second, even the *Fortune* 500 companies are rapidly adopting microcomputers as productivity tools for upper and middle managers and *knowledge workers.*

Which Computer Will Suit My Needs?

The issue is not which machine is fastest or prettiest. It is not generally a price issue, since most are competitively priced. It is one of "What am I going to do with a computer?" The key is *software* — the programs that are used to do the work. Other important issues are customer service and compatibility with existing computer systems. Can the new system transfer information to and from the company's central system? This might be important if you wish to use your local system as an input/output terminal to the central system. If your company's data processing (sometimes called management information systems) group has provided standard communications "interfaces," then almost all popular microcomputers will do the job.

The IBM Personal Computer, the Texas Instruments Professional Computer, DEC's Rainbow series, and Radio Shack's TRS-80 Models 16, 12, and II are all examples of relatively inexpensive systems that sell for $7,000 or less, depending on options such as memory, mass storage (disk systems), and communications options.

Choosing Options

As a rule of thumb, it is best to get as much memory as possible to ensure that your machine is compatible with the widest variety of software. More memory also makes the computer work faster, because it reduces the number of times the machine must "go to the well" to exchange data between memory and disk.

Disk capacity should be equal to the combined amount of information and programs that will be stored on the disk at any time during operation. Here again, the larger the storage capacity, the better off you will be. Floppy diskettes are often adequate for most routine tasks, particularly the high- density floppies, which hold from 320,000 to 1,000,000 *bytes* (characters) of storage. (Using 2,500 characters per 8 ½" by 11" page, 320,000 characters, or 320 kilobytes, of storage is approximately 125 pages.)

Another concern should be the layout and touch of a computer's keyboard and the resolution of the screen. The Texas Instruments Professional Computer features an extremely nice keyboard and an above-average quality display. Typists and "computer buffs" alike agree that the keyboard touch and layout is one of the best available. The resolution of the screen is 720 horizontal by 300 vertical "picture elements" (called *pixels*). This means that characters are very crisp and clear. A good way to check the resolution of a display is to look at 45-degree diagonal lines to see how "jagged" they appear. If they are fairly smooth, then the display should be satisfactory. If they have a "sawtooth" appearance, you may want to look for a better display, particularly if you plan to use graphics.

SYSTEM CONFIGURATION

There are several types of systems to select from today. Single-user desk-top microcomputers are the most common. But there are other configurations from which to choose. For example, some microcomputer systems can support two or more work stations. These are called *multitasking, multiuser* systems. Multiuser means that more than one user can use the system at the same time. Multitasking means that multiple tasks can be performed simultaneously. For example, a multitasking computer can run word processing, financial analysis, and database programs all at the same time. Companies that manufacture multiuser, multitasking microcomputers that can do this include Altos, Onyx, and Tandy.

EXCHANGING INFORMATION WITH OTHER WORK STATIONS AND SYSTEMS

An issue that should be included in your decision-making process is the ability of a system to communicate with other systems. This can include access to the company's central computer system, to computer systems belonging to customers or subcontractors, or to other work stations within your own department. The ability to take a document and transfer it to another computer-based system, such as a vendor's typesetter or your company's central computer system, may save thousands of dollars in labor, particularly if rekeyboarding is the primary alternative. Because the publications business is communications, you will find that modern data communications is a powerful tool in making your publications operation efficient and productive. The next few paragraphs describe telecommunications and local area networking.

Telecommunications

Telecommunications allows computers, which may be across town, in another city, or in another country, to exchange information for the price of a telephone call. All computers now on the market support telecommunications, but some do it better than others, depending on the quality of the communications software available. The key is to find what type of communications software is available for computer systems being considered and also, to determine what type of communications is used by those with whom you wish to communicate.

Categories of Telecommunications. There are two general categories of telecommunications. These are asynchronous, usually called TTY (for teletype), and binary-synchronous, often referred to as "bisynchronous." Within the bisynchronous category of telecommunication, there are several *protocols*, or data format specifications. These protocols generally have numbers assigned, such as 2780, 3780, 3270, and so on. Be sure to find out which protocols are available on systems under consideration. Then you can find out from those with whom you will be telecommunicating what they have and you can match them.

Data Transfer Speeds. TTY communications speeds generally range from 110 to 1200 bits per second, or *baud*, which is equivalent to 11 to 120 characters per second. The most common speed is 300 baud, or 30 characters per second. Bisychronous communications speeds generally range from 1,200 to 9,600 baud (120 to 960 characters per second). So the faster speed makes bisynchronous more attractive at first glance.

Error Checking and Data Integrity. In addition to data transfer speeds, data integrity is also an important consideration. TTY communications generally transfers information without error checking, although certain "smart" TTY software packages do perform some data checks. Bisynchronous communications, on the other hand, checks for data integrity. Each block of data, which is a 256-character group, is checked by the receiving computer. If there are any errors, a resend instruction is sent to the transmitting computer that tells it to send the last block again. When the block checks okay, the receiving computer stores it and instructs the transmitting computer to send the next block. This process continues until the entire document is transferred.

Telecommunications Selection. The advantage of error checking and speed, then, may persuade you to select the bisynchronous communications alternative. But, as in almost all spheres, you get what you pay for, and bisynchronous communications requires a larger initial investment in communications software and equipment. Because many choose to make a modest investment in communications, the most common is TTY. This means that you will probably require TTY to be compatible with most systems in use and bisynchronous communications to talk to those who can afford more sophisticated communications systems, which includes most large companies.

Local Area Networks

There are also local area network systems. A local area network (LAN) allows several computers to be connected together by a wire or cable. There are a number of types of LANs. These include *bus, twisted-pair, baseband,* and *broadband* technologies. A bus network is the slowest and least expensive. Twisted-pair networks, which include Tele-video's Mmmost system and Corvus' Omninet are also relatively inexpensive and operate at speeds of 1,000,000 bits per second (100,000 characters per second). Twisted-pair speeds are increasing, and some are running close to 4,000,000 bits per second at this writing.

One baseband network is the Ethernet, introduced by Xerox Corporation. Other companies, such as 3-COM, are manufacturing baseband systems for distribution into the microcomputer environment. The Ethernet can be used to interface microcomputers to large central computer systems and therefore is an alternative being considered by many electronic data processing groups.

The most expensive local area networking alternative is broadband. This technology accommodates digital computer data, audio, and even cable television signals over the same conductor. An example of a broadband local area network is Wang's Wangnet.

Local area networks can play an important role in the transfer and sharing of information between activities within your department. For example, you may have a central mass storage system within the department's network on which publications can be stored for other operations to access. Production status information, budget guidelines, specifications, and other management tools can be accessed by those who need them with the touch of a few keys. If you want to print a memo, it can be directed to a network-connected letter-quality printer. If it is a fast manuscript that is needed, it can be sent to the network's high-speed line or matrix printer. If there is a need to telecommunicate a document to another city, it can be routed to the network's telecommunications processor. The network, then, allows many work stations to share system resources, which eliminates the need for every desktop computer in the department to have dedicated mass storage, printers, and telecommunications.

SYSTEM APPLICATIONS

Applications include ways that a computer system can be applied to the publications process. This generally refers to software applications programs, including word processing, financial analysis, and database management. These are by no means the only ways that computers can be applied to the publications process, but they probably represent the top three in use today and are good ones to consider for initial adoption.

Word Processing

A professional writer's value is often measured in the quality and quantity of the work produced. The quality is measured on content value and accuracy. The quantity is measured by the number of pages produced per standard unit of time, such as pages per hour, week, or month.

Several years ago, writers were encouraged to use typewriters to speed their draft preparation. Those writers who used typewriters could generally produce more material than could those who prepared their drafts in longhand. In addition to being able to put words on paper faster with a typewriter, typed manuscript often eliminated the need for a draft typist and made the job of editing easier as well.

These same benefits also apply to modern word processing systems, only more so. Being able to prepare and modify text on the display screen of a word processing system without having to make corrections on paper speeds up the text entry process immensely. Some have estimated that word processing can be as much as five times faster than manual typing. This is particularly true for writers, who can assemble their thoughts on the screen and then cut and paste electronically to smooth things out.

Once the information is entered and "polished" by the writer, it can be printed on a typewriter quality (called *letter-quality*) or high-speed impact printer. The benefit of eliminating the draft typing phase and easier editing applies to the word processor in the same way that it applies to a typewriter. But there are still more advantages.

Word processors "capture" keystrokes on magnetic media, usually disks or tape, which means that the manuscript can be redisplayed, updated, refiled, and reprinted with minimum effort. Once all review comments are incorporated into the manuscript, the captured keystrokes can be transferred to the typesetting department, where only typesetting codes are added. Typesetting codes control type style, size, line lengths, space between lines (called *leading*), and other format parameters. These codes are normally inserted by a typesetting specialist. The ability to use the magnetically captured keystrokes saves the time that was once required to retype and proofread the entire document from scratch.

Cost Justification of Word Processing Systems. It is relatively easy to cost-justify the purchase or lease of a word processing system for a writer. If you consider that these systems are justified for secretarial personnel every day, then finding payback for a writer whose hourly rate may be twice that of a secretary should be less difficult. There are several cost justification elements to consider. These include

- Labor savings
- Quality improvement
- Cycle time

Labor. When determining labor savings, you should determine how much labor it takes to process a document using the existing system and how much you estimate it will take with improvements. The labor categories to consider should include

1. Writer
2. Editor
3. Draft typist
4. Proofreader
5. Reviewer
6. Typesetting specialist

In addition to labor categories, the number of passes that a document makes through the production process should also be counted. There could be as many as three or four passes, depending upon the number of reviews and changes. The following is how the first part of a sample cost-justification chart might look.

Description	TIME PER PAGE		SAVINGS PER PAGE	
	Before WP	After WP	Hours	Dollars
First pass				
Writer	4.0	3.5	0.5	$10.00
Draft typist	0.3	0.0	0.3	4.00
Proofreader	0.2	0.1	0.1	1.50
Editor	0.5	0.4	0.1	1.50
Reviewer	0.4	0.3	0.1	2.00
Typesetting specialist	0.7	0.2	0.5	7.00
Subtotal	6.1	4.5	1.6	$25.50
Subsequent passes				
Writer	0.5	0.3	0.2	$ 4.00
Draft typist	0.3	0.0	0.3	4.00
Editor	0.2	0.1	0.1	1.50
Reviewer	0.2	0.1	0.1	2.00
Typesetting specialist	0.2	0.1	0.1	1.40
Subtotal	1.4	0.6	0.8	$12.90

In this example the total savings per page for a publication having only one review pass would amount to $38.40. If a department generates an average of 200 new pages per month, the monthly saving would be

200 pages $\times$ $38.40 = $7,680.00 per month

Annualized, this would amount to

12 $\times$ $7,680.00 = $92,160.00 per year

These amounts would vary in proportion to the number of passes that a page makes through the publications process and with the labor rates.

Another method used to cost-justify word processing systems is to list the word processing feature and determine how much time each function can save. The following list shows this approach.

Function	Writer	Editor	Draft Typist	Proof-reader	Reviewer	Type-set
Editing	0.5	0.2	0.3	0.05	0.1	0.1
Spelling	0.1	0.1	0.1	0.1	0.1	0.0
Global replace	0.05	0.0	0.05	0.0	0.05	0.05
Hours	0.65	0.3	0.45	0.15	0.25	0.15
Rate	20.00	15.00	10.00	12.00	20.00	14.00
Savings/page	13.00	4.50	4.50	1.80	5.00	2.25
Total savings per page	$31.05					

Word Processing System Features. Table 11-1 contains descriptions of typical word processing features. When looking at word processing systems, a comparison matrix can be prepared to compare systems. The matrix can help determine which system best suits the needs of your department. Such a comparison matrix exists in Chapter 9 of *The Word Processing Handbook*, a Prentice-Hall publication that describes the selection and profitable use of word processing systems in the office.

TABLE 11-1 Common Word Processing System Features

Feature	Description
Bold print	Allows characters to be bold printed using multiple strikes.
Centering	Automatically centers one or more words between the right- and left-hand margin or over a specific location on the page.
Column editing	Allows deletion, insertion, moving, and copying of columns of text.
Copy (or duplicate)	Allows text to be copied in other locations of a document. A table heading may be duplicated several times eliminating the need to retype it for every page of a table.
Decimal tab	Automatically aligns decimals (periods) in a vertical column. Used for financial and mathematical document alignment.
Delete	Removes (deletes) text to be erased from a document. Following text automatically fills the space vacated by the erased text.
Document assembly	Assembles selected passages ("boilerplate") from existing documents to form a new document.
Double strike	Strikes paper twice; used for printing multiple-part forms and carbons.
Double underscore	Allows designated text to be double underscored.
Global search (find)	System automatically locates a specified text string.
Global search and replace	System automatically locates a specified text string and replaces it with another.
Global delete	System automatically locates a specified text string and deletes it.
Hyphenation	The hyphenation feature allows words located at the right margin to be automatically hyphenated. Some systems are semiautomatic, where the operator must make the hyphenation decision. Others use hyphenation dictionaries and break and hyphenate words automatically.

TABLE 11-1   Common Word Processing System Features (Cont.)

Feature	Description
Indent	Indents to a tab and holds left margin at the indent setting until a subsequent indent level is set or the RETURN key is pressed.
Insert	Allows text to be inserted in existing text. For example, a character, word, sentence, paragraph, or page can be inserted in the middle of an existing document.
List/merge	System merges a list of variables, such as a mailing list, with a base document. (Popular in form letter operations.)
Move	Allows text to be moved from one location to another. For example, a sentence or paragraph can be picked up from one location and laid down in another.
Overprint	Overprints two characters at the same location, such as a 0 and / to produce Ø.
Right-hand justification	Automatically inserts space to produce an even (smooth) right-hand margin.
Spelling dictionary	System searches file for dictionary mismatches, which will be misspelled words or typographical errors. If technical terms or new words are used, many systems allow them to be added to the dictionary.
Stop code	Allows printer to be stopped to change type font (such as from text face to italic).
Strike-through	Marks out a passage of text with a designated character, such as a dash, slash mark, or capital "ex" (X).
Strikeover	Allows characters to be replaced by typing over them.
Tab	Allows standard typewriter-like tabbing. Used for preparing tables and charts.
Underscore (underline)	Allows designated text to be underlined.

Many other word processing features are available. To describe them all is beyond the scope of this book. However, you may wish to refer to *The Illustrated Word Processing Dictionary*, Prentice-Hall, Inc., 1982. This book is a word processing tutorial that describes word processing features in detail and illustrates their use with diagrams of screens and text manipulation.

Word Processor to Typesetter. Another area of value is the word processor-to-typesetter link. By using the proper interface, word processors can communicate files directly to photocomposers.

For example, a word processing system can be connected directly to a photocomposer. Documents can be created and coded for typesetting using the powerful text editing features of a word processor. Once coded and filed, documents can be telecommunicated, either over telephone lines or by means of direct cable connection, to the typesetting system. The received document is stored on magnetic disk in the photo-composer. Next, it can be checked by the typesetting operator on a *preview* system, which displays a facsimile of output documents on a display screen to ensure that line breaks, type sizes, centering, and other format concerns are correct. Without a preview system, a document must be typeset before it can be checked. This takes time and material, and often a preview system can be cost-justified based on the time and material lost in rework.

Another approach is to typeset a proof copy on a high-speed laser printer. The fast speed and use of inexpensive bond paper saves the time and material used by conventional photocomposers.

This book was typed and coded on a microcomputer. The files were telecommunicated to an Autologic APS-5 photo-composer. The productivity gained from this arrangement is impressive when compared with conventional means. Rekeyboarding, extensive proofreading, author corrections, and comment incorporation are either completely eliminated or are minimized through the use of modern technology.

Financial Analysis

All businesses that are concerned with such activities as cost estimating, budgeting, and financial reporting can benefit from financial analysis software. Specifically, electronic spreadsheets are programs that provide universal planning forms on the display screen of a microcomputer. Spreadsheets, sometimes called "worksheets," such as Visicorp's Visicalc, Sorcim's Supercalc, MicroPro's CalcStar, and Microsoft's Multiplan are all useful tools. If you are not familiar with the operation of a spreadsheet, you should read the next few paragraphs to understand how you might use one.

Spreadsheet Format.   A spreadsheet is divided into numbered rows and columns, like most paper-based financial planning sheets. Figure 11-1 illustrates a typical spreadsheet format.

```
        A   |   B   |   C   |   D   |   E   |   F   |
  1
  2
  3
  4
  5
  6
  7
```

FIGURE 11-1   Typical Spreadsheet Format

The intersection of a row and column is referred to as a *cell*. For example, the upper left-hand cell is A1. Cell C3 is in column C, row 3. The total size of a spreadsheet is normally around 68 columns by 255 rows. Using these numbers, the lower right-hand cell would be labeled BP255, where columns range from A to Z, AA to AZ, and BA to BP. Because most display screens are only 25 lines by 80 characters wide, looking at the spreadsheet is like looking through a window. You can move to different portions of the spreadsheet by scrolling the spreadsheet past the "window" with the cursor control keys or mouse, depending on the type of system you are using.

You should not be led to believe that every cell within a spreadsheet can be occupied by a value. There would be 17,340 entries in a 68-column by 255- row sheet. However, the system's memory will generally limit you to between 600 and 2,000 cell entries, depending on memory. There are a few "virtual memory" systems, however, that exchange data between the system's memory and disk storage to expand the effective size of the spreadsheet.

Spreadsheet Entries. Within the cells of a spreadsheet, numerical values, text, or equations can be entered. Numerical values are usually dollars, hours, production units, percentages, and similar entries. Text entries can be any kind of descriptive label desired. Equations are used to establish fixed relationships between cell entries. Let us look at the following spreadsheet example in Figure 11-2 to demonstrate these.

In this example, column D is used to multiply the units entered in column B times the cost values entered in column C. Overhead factors are entered into column E, and column F is used to multiply the overhead factors by the subtotals derived in column D. The results of the display would appear as those shown in Figure 11-3.

	A	B	C	D	E	F
1	Descrip	Units	Cost	Subtotal	Overhead	Total
2	Text Pg	98.00	16.25	B2*C2	1.75	D2*E2
3	Tab Pg	22.00	23.75	B3*C3	1.75	D3*E3
4	Line Art	11.00	45.00	B4*C4	1.80	D4*E4
5	Tone Art	6.00	42.50	B5*C5	2.00	D5*E5
6		-------		-------		-------
7	Totals	SUM(B2:B5)		SUM(D2:D5)		SUM(F2:F5)

FIGURE 11-2   Typical Spreadsheet Entries

Other relationships could be established to determine dollars per page, the average overhead rate, the percentage that each type of page represents within a book, and so on.

Once a spreadsheet is designed, it can be saved and used over and over. New numbers can be tried by simply positioning the cursor over the target cells and typing them in. The derived values change as new numbers are entered, giving instant answers. This is what makes spreadsheets the highest selling software on the market today. The ability to play "what if" games, changing values and seeing answers in

	A	B	C	D	E	F
1	Descrip	Units	Cost	Subtotal	Overhead	Total
2	Text Pg	98.00	16.25	1,592.50	1.75	2,786.88
3	Tab Pg	22.00	23.75	522.50	1.75	914.38
4	Line Art	11.00	45.00	495.00	1.80	891.00
5	Tone Art	6.00	42.50	255.00	2.00	510.00
6		-------		-------		-------
7	Totals	137.00		2,865.00		5,101.38

FIGURE 11-3   Typical Spreadsheet Display

a fraction of a second eliminates the drudgery of calculating, writing, changing, recalculating, erasing, and rewriting. Now all that is required is a few simple keystrokes. Once satisfied with the displayed results, the spreadsheet can be printed and saved in paper form with other financial records. Spreadsheets can also be combined with word processed text files to prepare financial report, forecast, or cost proposal documents.

Database and File Management Packages

The third category of software to be described is database and file management programs. As are word processors and spreadsheets, there are several database and file management packages available. Examples are Ashton-Tate's dBASE II, MicroPro International's DataStar and InfoStar, and Software Publishing's PFS: File and PFS:Report. The balance of this section describes database management functions and uses.

What Is a Database?   A database is a collection of records. An example of a record is an employee record in a personnel database that is made up of discrete fields of information, such as name, address, job grade, labor category, or salary rate. A database file, then, is made up of records, and records are made up of fields. Following is an example of a publications job database, where each record represents a book's production status.

Field	Description	Type	Width	Decimals
001	Job:No	C	008	
002	Title	C	030	
003	Customer	C	020	
004	Charge	C	009	
005	Start	C	008	
006	Finish	C	008	
007	Status	C	002	
008	Est:Cost	N	009	2
009	Act:Cost	N	009	2
010	Complete	L	001	

Field   A discrete type of entry within a record. In this example there are 10 fields

Description   An eight-character descriptive field name

Type   Field content type, which can be character (C), numeric (N), or logical (L)

Width   The number of characters or numbers and decimal point that can be entered into a field

Decimals   The number of decimal places in a numeric field

Use of Database Information.   In the sample database, each record contains information about a specific publications job. Job numbers, descriptions, customer contact data, schedule and cost information, current status, and other data can be entered about each job. Reports can be listed on a printer or displayed on a computer display screen to determine the status of every job in the database. The reports can be designed to provide information about projects in specific production areas by listing only those jobs with a predesignated two-digit work area status code. For example, writing might be WR, editing ED, typesetting TS, illustrating IL, review RV, printing PR, and so forth. In dBASE II, the command

```
DISPLAY FOR STATUS = "ED"
```

would display every job in editing. The command

```
DISPLAY FOR STATUS = "WR" .AND. STATUS = "ED"
```

would display every job in writing and editing.

Completed jobs can be eliminated from the report by listing only those jobs with a logical entry of "not" complete. Conversely, completed jobs can be listed by selecting only those jobs that have a complete status. Other valuable information, such as jobs in backlog or cost versus actual, can be obtained.

Although this is a relatively simple database, it demonstrates how a database package can be used in publications production control. The addition of a few more fields, such as cost by labor category and cycle-time datapoints, extends such a database into a sophisticated production planning and monitoring tool. The addition of these fields could provide statistical information used to establish and refine production cost and schedule standards.

Summary

As you can see, a database manager can be a powerful tool. There are literally hundreds of applications that can be built around a database management system in a publications environment. Cost-estimating data, equipment and supplies, inventory control, petty cash records, accounts receivable, personnel files, customer records, and many other database management applications are possible.

DICTATION EQUIPMENT

Dictation equipment is another type of word processing equipment that can be used to a writer's advantage. The use of recording and transcription equipment was mentioned in Chapters 2 and 4. The benefits were mentioned briefly. To help illustrate the value of dictation equipment, some personal experiences are related.

From 1979 through 1981 I was involved in researching and writing three management development books for a large, multinational corporation. These books included subjects such as profit and loss entity management; marketing; institutionalizing a productivity and quality culture; and selecting, installing, and operating international manufacturing plants. All three books were written with heavy use of a microcassette tape recorder and transcriber.

The tape recorder and many boxes of cassettes were carried all over the world. Because of power differences from country to country, a good supply of 1.5-volt penlight (A cell) batteries were carried on the first trip. I found that the batteries became weak after several hours of recording. The weak batteries caused the recorder's motor to slow down, making transcription difficult due to variances in the transcription speed.

To counter this problem, I purchased a step-down transformer and a set of electrical outlet adapters for use in the Far East, Europe, and South America, where primary house power is 220 volts AC. Equipped with this equipment and a portable power supply unit, I was able to eliminate the battery problem.

The dictation equipment was used to record planned interviews with subject matter experts in a variety of locations. Eighty-six hours of dictation were gathered on one book. This book turned out to be "pure gold," with tips and advice in the form of direct quotations from experienced managers located all over the world. Needless to say, without the help of a tape recorder, the direct quotations would have lost both color and credibility through paraphrase. In addition, the time saved in interviews was immense. Information capture through dictation was several orders of magnitude more efficient than it would have been with paper and pencil.

Once back at the office, the transcription process began. Although some months and perhaps 100,000 miles had passed between the early interviews and the start of the transcription process, the taped voices, their accents, inflections, and passions took me back. As I typed their words, my mind's eye looked at them. I visualized their facial expressions and gestures. Even the surroundings came back: the wall color, furnishings, and the view through the window. I was struck with another advantage of dictation — almost-total recall. The ability to relive the "feel" as well as the words — the ability to reproduce faithfully the interview in every detail. Hence, dictation made the collection and reproduction processes more efficient and more accurate.

The transcription process took several months, using a word processing system to capture the transcribed material. All text was stored on magnetic media, by subject category. By doing the transcription personally, I was able to eliminate an intermediate transcription step by a draft typist. More important, I was able to "rough out" the text in close to final form on the first pass.

Once the transcription process was completed, each chapter and section was reorganized and edited into a manuscript. The single-spaced, typed manuscript was around 750 pages. Needless to say, a book of this size could have never been achieved by one writer without the aid of dictation and word processing equipment. I shudder to think how difficult the undertaking would have been with a pencil and note pad.

SUMMARY

This book has presented both details and overviews about a lot of things that have to do with the business side of technical writing. How to do it, how to do it right, and how to do it better. It is my sincere wish that you have found value here and that you will keep the book close at hand, using the examples as models for your own needs.

REVIEW QUESTIONS

1. How may a professional writer's productivity be measured?

2. What two categories of computer systems followed *mainframes*?

3. What are some important considerations when shopping for a computer?

4. What is the difference between *telecommunications* and a *local area network*?

5. Describe the word processing *global search and replace* function.

6. Describe the *stop code* function.

7. What is meant by *document assembly*?

8. What benefits can be realized by having a spelling dictionary?

9. What are some of the benefits derived from having a direct word processing to typesetting system interface?

10. What is a *spreadsheet*?

11. How might a spreadsheet be used to help a publications manager?

12. What is meant by a database?

13. Define the terms *file*, *record*, and *field*.

14. Describe the difference between character, numerical, and logical fields.

Index